Swift 3 Game Development

Second Edition

Embrace the mobile gaming revolution by creating popular iOS games with Swift 3.0

Stephen Haney

BIRMINGHAM - MUMBAI

Swift 3 Game Development

Second Edition

First published: July 2015

Second edition: February 2017

Production reference: 1310117

Published by Packt Publishing Ltd.
Livery Place
35 Livery Street
Birmingham
B32PB, UK.
ISBN 978-1-78712-775-3

www.packtpub.com

Credits

Author	**Copy Editor**
Stephen Haney	Safis Editing
Reviewer	**Project Coordinator**
Giordano Scalzo	Ulhas Kambali
Commissioning Editor	**Proofreader**
Ashwin Nair	Safis Editing
Acquisition Editor	**Indexer**
Reshma Raman	Rekha Nair
Content Development Editor	**Graphics**
Onkar Wani	Abhinash Sahu
Technical Editor	**Production Coordinator**
Rashil Shah	Nilesh Mohite

About the Author

Stephen Haney has written two books on iOS game development. He began his programming journey at the age of 8 years on a dusty, ancient laptop using BASIC. He has been fascinated with building software and games ever since. Now well versed in multiple languages, he enjoys programming as a creative outlet the most. He believes that indie game development is an art form-- an amazing combination of visual, auditory, and psychological challenges--rewarding to both the player and the creator.

He enjoyed writing this book and sincerely hopes that it directly furthers your career or hobby.

Thank you to my wonderful father, mother, and sister for their patience as I write and work, and also to my friends: Geoff, Robert, Justin, Jessie, Devin, Jason, Ben, Chris, Anna, and Shane, among others. I love you all!

About the Reviewer

Giordano Scalzo is a developer with 20 years of programming experience since the days of the ZX Spectrum.

He has worked in C++, Java, .NET, Ruby, Python, and in a ton of other languages he has forgotten the names of. After years of backend development, over the past five years, Giordano has done extensive development for iOS, releasing more than 20 apps that he wrote for clients and enterprise applications on his own.

Currently, he is a contractor in London where, through his company--Effective Code Ltd (`http://effectivecode.co.uk`)--he delivers code for iOS, aiming at quality and reliability.

In his spare time, when he is not crafting retro game clones for iOS, he writes and shares his thoughts on `http://giordanoscalzo.com`.

> *I'd like to thank my better half, Valentina, who lovingly supports me in everything I do: without you, none of this would have been possible. Thanks to my bright future, Mattia and Luca, for giving me lots of smiles and hugs when I needed them. Finally, my gratitude goes to my mum and my dad, who encouraged my curiosity and supported me to follow my passions, which began one day when they bought me a ZX Spectrum.*

www.PacktPub.com

For support files and downloads related to your book, please visit www.PacktPub.com.

Did you know that Packt offers eBook versions of every book published, with PDF and ePub files available? You can upgrade to the eBook version at www.PacktPub.com and as a print book customer, you are entitled to a discount on the eBook copy. Get in touch with us at service@packtpub.com for more details.

At www.PacktPub.com, you can also read a collection of free technical articles, sign up for a range of free newsletters and receive exclusive discounts and offers on Packt books and eBooks.

https://www.packtpub.com/mapt

Get the most in-demand software skills with Mapt. Mapt gives you full access to all Packt books and video courses, as well as industry-leading tools to help you plan your personal development and advance your career.

Why subscribe?

- Fully searchable across every book published by Packt
- Copy and paste, print, and bookmark content
- On demand and accessible via a web browser

Customer Feedback

Thank you for purchasing this Packt book. We take our commitment to improving our content and products to meet your needs seriously--that's why your feedback is so valuable. Whatever your feelings about your purchase, please consider leaving a review on this book's Amazon page. Not only will this help us, more importantly it will also help others in the community to make an informed decision about the resources that they invest in to learn.

You can also review for us on a regular basis by joining our reviewers' club. **If you're interested in joining, or would like to learn more about the benefits we offer, please contact us**: customerreviews@packtpub.com.

Table of Contents

Preface

There has never been a better time to be a game developer. The App Store provides a unique opportunity to distribute your ideas to a massive audience. Also, now Swift 3 has arrived! Apple's Swift language is maturing and hitting its stride in version 3. Whether you are new to game development or looking to add to your expertise, I think you will enjoy making games with Swift.

With this book, my goal is to share a fundamental knowledge of Swift and SpriteKit. We will work through a complete example game so that you learn every step of the Swift development process. Once you finish this text, you will be comfortable designing and publishing your own game ideas to the App Store from start to finish.

Please reach out to me for any questions and share your game creations:

E-mail: stephen@joyfulgames.io

Twitter: @sdothaney

The first chapter explores some of Swift's best features. Let's get started!

What this book covers

Chapter 1, *Designing Games with Swift*, introduces you to the best features of Swift, outlines what is new in Swift 3, helps you set up your development environment, and launches your first SpriteKit project.

Chapter 2, *Sprites, Camera, Action!*, teaches you the basics of drawing and animating with Swift. You will draw sprites, import textures into your project, and center the camera on the main character.

Chapter 3, *Mix in the Physics*, covers the physics simulation fundamentals: physics bodies, impulses, forces, gravity, collisions, and more.

Chapter 4, *Adding Controls*, explores the various methods of mobile game controls: device tilt and touch input. We will also improve the camera and core gameplay of our example game.

Chapter 5, *Spawning Enemies, Coins, and Power-ups*, introduces the cast of characters we use in our example game and shows you how to create custom classes for each NPC type.

Chapter 6, *Generating a Never-Ending World*, explores the SpriteKit scene editor, builds encounters for the example game, and creates a system to loop encounters endlessly.

Chapter 7, *Implementing Collision Events*, delves into advanced physics simulation topics and adds custom events when sprites collide.

Chapter 8, *Polishing to a Shine – HUD, Parallax Backgrounds, Particles, and More*, adds the extra fun that makes every game shine. In this chapter, you will learn to create parallax backgrounds, learn about SpriteKit's particle emitters, and add a heads-up display overlay to your games.

Chapter 9, *Adding Menus and Sounds*, builds a basic menu system and illustrates two methods of playing sounds in your games.

Chapter 10, *Standing Out in the Crowd with Advanced Features*, shows you how to combine the techniques you have learned to build advanced gameplay systems.

Chapter 11, *Choosing a Monetization Strategy*, outlines the strategies available to indie developers who want to make money from their games.

Chapter 12, *Integrating with Game Center*, links our example game to the Apple Game Center for leaderboards, achievements, and friendly challenges.

Chapter 13, *Ship It! Preparing for the App Store and Publication*, covers the essentials of packaging your game and submitting it to the App Store.

What you need for this book

This book uses the Xcode IDE, version 8.2.1 (Swift 3). If you use a different version of Xcode, you will likely encounter syntax differences; Apple is constantly upgrading Swift's syntax. You can use Xcode's Edit > Convert > To Current Swift Syntax to update the code examples in this book to a newer version of Xcode.

Visit `https://developer.apple.com/xcode/` to download Xcode.

You will need an Apple developer account to integrate your apps with the Game Center and submit your games to the App Store.

Who this book is for

If you wish to create and publish fun iOS games using Swift, this book is for you. You should be familiar with basic programming concepts. However, no prior game development or Apple ecosystem experience is required.

Conventions

In this book, you will find a number of text styles that distinguish between different kinds of information. Here are some examples of these styles and an explanation of their meaning.

Code words in text, database table names, folder names, filenames, file extensions, pathnames, dummy URLs, user input, and Twitter handles are shown as follows: "The compiler will expect your variables to be of a certain type (int, string, and so on) and will throw a compile-time error if you try to assign a value of a different type."

A block of code is set as follows:

```
import SpriteKit

class GameScene: SKScene {
 override func didMove(to view: SKView) {
 }
}
```

New terms and **important words** are shown in bold. Words that you see on the screen, for example, in menus or dialog boxes, appear in the text like this: "Launch Xcode and navigate to **File | New | Project**."

Warnings or important notes appear in a box like this.

Tips and tricks appear like this.

Reader feedback

Feedback from our readers is always welcome. Let us know what you think about this book-what you liked or disliked. Reader feedback is important for us as it helps us develop titles that you will really get the most out of. To send us general feedback, simply e-mail feedback@packtpub.com, and mention the book's title in the subject of your message. If there is a topic that you have expertise in and you are interested in either writing or contributing to a book, see our author guide at www.packtpub.com/authors.

Customer support

Now that you are the proud owner of a Packt book, we have a number of things to help you to get the most from your purchase.

Downloading the example code

You can download the example code files for this book from your account at http://www.packtpub.com. If you purchased this book elsewhere, you can visit http://www.packtpub.com/support and register to have the files e-mailed directly to you.

You can download the code files by following these steps:

1. Log in or register to our website using your e-mail address and password.
2. Hover the mouse pointer on the **SUPPORT** tab at the top.
3. Click on **Code Downloads & Errata**.
4. Enter the name of the book in the **Search** box.
5. Select the book for which you're looking to download the code files.
6. Choose from the drop-down menu where you purchased this book from.
7. Click on **Code Download**.

Once the file is downloaded, please make sure that you unzip or extract the folder using the latest version of:

- WinRAR / 7-Zip for Windows
- Zipeg / iZip / UnRarX for Mac
- 7-Zip / PeaZip for Linux

The code bundle for the book is also hosted on GitHub at `https://github.com/PacktPubl ishing/-Swift-3-Game-Development`. We also have other code bundles from our rich catalog of books and videos available at `https://github.com/PacktPublishing/`. Check them out!

Downloading the color images of this book

We also provide you with a PDF file that has color images of the screenshots/diagrams used in this book. The color images will help you better understand the changes in the output. You can download this file from `https://www.packtpub.com/sites/default/files/down loads/Swift3GameDevelopmentSecondEdition_ColorImages.pdf`.

Errata

Although we have taken every care to ensure the accuracy of our content, mistakes do happen. If you find a mistake in one of our books-maybe a mistake in the text or the code-we would be grateful if you could report this to us. By doing so, you can save other readers from frustration and help us improve subsequent versions of this book. If you find any errata, please report them by visiting `http://www.packtpub.com/submit-errata`, selecting your book, clicking on the **Errata Submission Form** link, and entering the details of your errata. Once your errata are verified, your submission will be accepted and the errata will be uploaded to our website or added to any list of existing errata under the Errata section of that title.

To view the previously submitted errata, go to `https://www.packtpub.com/books/conten t/support` and enter the name of the book in the search field. The required information will appear under the **Errata** section.

Piracy

Piracy of copyrighted material on the Internet is an ongoing problem across all media. At Packt, we take the protection of our copyright and licenses very seriously. If you come across any illegal copies of our works in any form on the Internet, please provide us with the location address or website name immediately so that we can pursue a remedy.

Please contact us at `copyright@packtpub.com` with a link to the suspected pirated material.

We appreciate your help in protecting our authors and our ability to bring you valuable content.

Questions

If you have a problem with any aspect of this book, you can contact us at questions@packtpub.com, and we will do our best to address the problem.

1
Designing Games with Swift

Apple's newest version of its flagship programming language, **Swift 3**, is the perfect choice for game developers. As it matures, Swift is realizing its opportunity to be something special, a revolutionary tool for app creators. Swift is the gateway for developers to create the next big game in the Apple ecosystem. We have only started to explore the wonderful potential of mobile gaming and Swift is the modernization we need for our toolset. Swift is fast, safe, current, and attractive to developers coming from other languages. Whether you are new to the Apple world, or a seasoned veteran of **Objective-C**, I think you will enjoy making games with Swift.

Apple's website states the following:

> *"Swift is a successor to the C and Objective-C languages."*

My goal in this book is to guide you step-by-step through the creation of a 2D game for iPhones and iPads. We will start with installing the necessary software, working through each layer of game development, ultimately publishing our new game to the **App Store**.

We will also have some fun along the way! We aim to create an endless flyer game featuring a magnificent flying penguin named **Pierre**. What is an endless flyer? Picture hit games like iCopter, Flappy Bird, Whale Trail, Jetpack Joyride, and many more–the list is quite long.

Endless flyer games are popular on the App Store and the genre necessitates that we cover many reusable components of 2D game design. I will show you how to modify our mechanics to create many different game styles. My hope is that our demo project will serve as a template for your own creative works. Before you know it, you will be publishing your own game ideas using the techniques we explore together.

In this chapter, we will cover the following topics:

- Why you will love Swift
- What you will learn in this book
- New in Swift 3
- Setting up your development environment
- Creating your first Swift game

Why you will love Swift

Swift, as a modern programming language, benefits from the collective experience of the programming community; it combines the best parts of other languages and avoids poor design decisions. Here are a few of my favorite Swift features:

- **Beautiful syntax:** Swift's syntax is modern and approachable, regardless of your existing programming experience. Apple have balanced syntax with structure to make Swift concise and readable.
- **Interoperability:** Swift can plug directly into your existing projects and run side by side with your Objective-C code.
- **Strong typing:** Swift is a strongly typed language. This means the compiler will catch more bugs at compile time, instead of when your users are playing your game! The compiler will expect your variables to be of a certain type (`int`, `string`, and so on) and will throw a compile-time error if you try to assign a value of a different type. While this may seem rigid if you are coming from a weakly typed language, the added structure results in safer, more reliable code.
- **Smart type inference:** To make things easier, **type inference** will automatically detect the types of your variables and constants based upon their initial value. You do not need to explicitly declare a type for your variables. Swift is smart enough to infer variable types in most expressions.
- **Automatic memory management:** As the Apple Swift developer guide states, *"memory management just works in Swift"*. Swift uses a method called **Automatic Reference Counting** (**ARC**) to manage your game's memory usage. Besides a few edge cases, you can rely on Swift to safely clean up and turn off the lights.
- **An even playing field:** One of my favorite things about Swift is how quickly the language is gaining mainstream adoption. We are all learning and growing together and there is a tremendous opportunity to break new ground.

- **Open source:** From version 2.2 onwards, Apple made Swift open source, curating it through the website www.swift.org, and launched a package manager with Swift 3. This is a welcome change, as it fosters greater community involvement and a larger ecosystem of third-party tools and add-ons. Eventually, we should see Swift migrate to new platforms.

Prerequisites

I will try to make this text easy to understand for all skill levels:

- I will assume you are brand new to Swift as a language
- This book requires no prior game development experience, though it will help
- I will assume you have a fundamental understanding of common programming concepts

What you will learn in this book

By the end of this book, you will be capable of creating and publishing your own iOS games. You will know how to combine the techniques we learned to create your own style of game and you will be well prepared to dive into more advanced topics with a solid foundation in 2D game design.

Embracing SpriteKit

SpriteKit is Apple's 2D game development framework and your main tool for iOS game design. SpriteKit will handle the mechanics of our graphics rendering, physics, and sound playback. As far as game development frameworks go, SpriteKit is a terrific choice. It is built and supported by Apple and thus integrates perfectly with Xcode and iOS. You will learn to be highly proficient with SpriteKit as we will be using it exclusively in our demo game.

We will learn to use SpriteKit to power the mechanics of our game in the following ways:

- Animating our player, enemies, and power-ups
- Painting and moving side-scrolling environments
- Playing sounds and music
- Applying physics such as gravity and impulses for movement
- Handling collisions between game objects

Reacting to player input

The control schemes in mobile games must be inventive. Mobile hardware forces us to simulate traditional controller inputs, such as directional pads and multiple buttons, on the screen. This takes up valuable visible area and provides less precision and feedback than with physical devices. Many games operate with only a single input method: a single tap anywhere on the screen. We will learn how to make the best of mobile input and explore new forms of control by sensing device motion and tilt.

Structuring your game code

It is important to write well-structured code that is easy to re-use and modify as your game design inevitably changes. You will often find mechanical improvements as you develop and test your games and you will thank yourself for a clean working environment. Though there are many ways to approach this topic, we will explore some best practices to build an organized system with classes, protocols, inheritance, and composition.

Building UI/menus/levels

We will learn to switch between scenes in our game with a menu screen. We will cover the basics of user experience design and menu layout as we build our demo game.

Integrating with Game Center

Game Center is Apple's built-in social gaming network. Your game can tie into Game Center to store and share high scores and achievements. We will learn how to register for Game Center, tie it into our code, and create a fun achievement system.

Maximizing fun

If you are like me, you will have dozens of ideas for games floating around your head. Ideas come easily, but designing fun gameplay is difficult! It is common to find that your ideas need gameplay enhancements once you see your design in action. We will look at how to avoid dead-ends and see your project through to the finish line. Plus, I will share my tips and tricks to ensure your game will bring joy to your players.

Crossing the finish line

Creating a game is an experience you will treasure. Sharing your hard work will only sweeten the satisfaction. Once our game is polished and ready for public consumption, we will navigate the App Store submission process together. You will end up feeling confident in your ability to create games with Swift and bring them to market in the App Store.

Monetizing your work

Game development is a fun and rewarding process, even without compensation, but the potential exists to start a career, or side job, selling games on the App Store. Successfully promoting and marketing your game is an important task. I will outline your options and start you down the path to monetization.

New in Swift 3

The biggest feature in Swift 3 is syntax compatibility and stability. Apple is trying to refine its young, shifting language into its final foundational shape. Each successive update of Swift has introduced breaking syntax changes that made older code incompatible with the newest version of Swift; this is very inconvenient for developers. Going forward, Swift 3 aims to reach maturity and maintain source compatibility with future releases of the language. Swift 3 also features the following:

- A package manager that will help grow the ecosystem
- A more consistent, readable API and API guidelines that often result in less code for the same result
- Improved tooling and bug fixes in the IDE, Xcode
- Many small syntax improvements in consistency and clarity

Swift has already made tremendous steps forward as a powerful, young language. Now Apple is working on polishing Swift into a mature, production-ready tool. The overall developer experience improves with Swift 3.

Setting up your development environment

Learning a new development environment can be a roadblock. Luckily, Apple provides some excellent tools for iOS developers. We will start our journey by installing Xcode.

Introducing and installing Xcode

Xcode is Apple's **Integrated Development Environment** (**IDE**). You will need Xcode to create your game projects, write and debug your code, and build your project for the App Store. Xcode also comes bundled with an iOS simulator to test your game on virtualized iPhones and iPads on your computer.

Apple praises Xcode as *"an incredibly productive environment for building amazing apps for Mac, iPhone, and iPad"*.

To install Xcode, search for Xcode in the AppStore, or visit `http://developer.apple.com` and select **Developer** and then **Xcode**.

 Swift is continually evolving and each new Xcode release brings changes to Swift. If you run into errors because Swift has changed, you can always use Xcode's built-in syntax update tool. Simply use Xcode's **Edit** | **Convert to Latest Syntax** option to update your code.

Xcode performs common IDE features to help you write better, faster code. If you have used IDEs in the past, then you are probably familiar with autocompletion, live error highlighting, running and debugging a project, and using a project manager pane to create and organize your files. However, any new program can seem overwhelming at first. We will walk through some common interface functions over the next few pages. I have also found tutorial videos on YouTube to be particularly helpful if you are stuck. Most common search queries result in helpful videos.

Creating our first Swift game

Do you have Xcode installed? Let's see some game code in action in the simulator!

We will start by creating a new project in Xcode. For our demo game, we will create a side-scrolling endless flyer featuring an astonishing flying penguin named *Pierre*. I am going to name this project *Pierre Penguin Escapes the Antarctic*, but feel free to name your project whatever you like. Follow these steps to create a new project in Xcode:

1. Launch Xcode and navigate to **File | New | Project**.
2. You will see a screen asking you to select a template for your new project. Select **iOS | Application** in the left pane, and **Game** in the right pane. It should look like this:

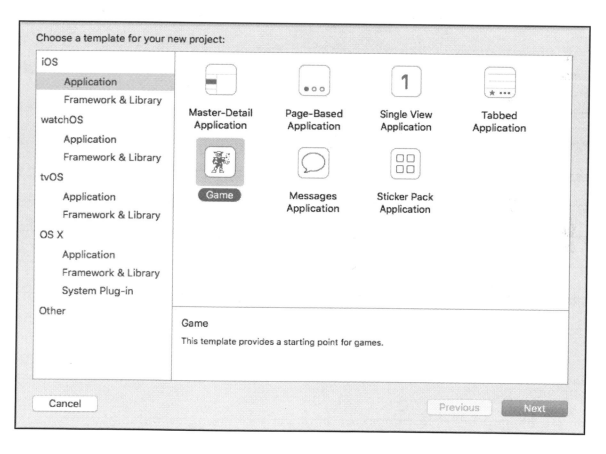

3. Once you have selected **Game**, click **Next**. The following screen asks us to enter some basic information about our project. Don't worry; we are almost at the fun bit. Fill in the **Product Name** field with the name of your game.

4. Let's fill in the **Team** field. Do you have an active Apple developer account? If not, you can skip over the **Team** field for now. If you do, your **Team** is your developer account. Click **Add Team** and Xcode will open the accounts screen where you can log in. Enter your developer credentials, as shown in the following screenshot:

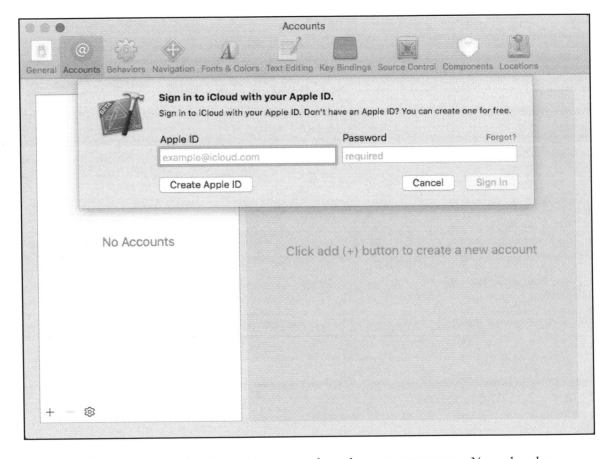

5. Once you're authenticated, you can close the accounts screen. Your developer account should appear in the **Team** dropdown.

6. You will want to pick a meaningful **Organization Name** and **Organization Identifier** when you create your own games for publication. Your **Organization Name** is the name of your game development studio. For me, that is Joyful Games. By convention, your Organization Identifier should follow a reverse domain name style. I will use io.JoyfulGames since my website is JoyfulGames.io.

7. After you filled out the name fields, be sure to select **Swift** for the **Language**, **SpriteKit** for **Game Technology**, and **Universal** for **Devices**.

8. For now, uncheck **Integrate GameplayKit**, uncheck **Include Unit Tests**, and uncheck **Include UI Tests**. We will not use these features in our demo game. Here are my final project settings:

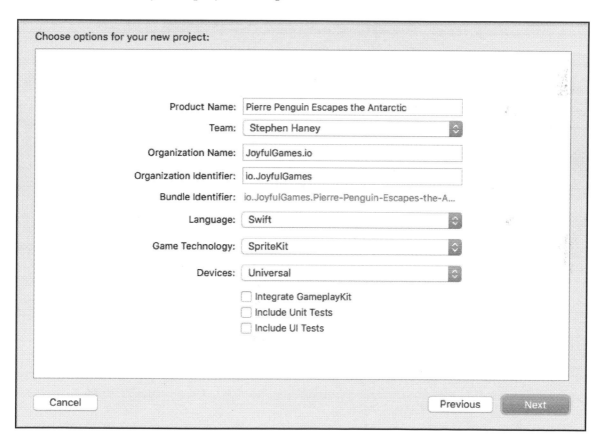

9. Click **Next** and you will see the final dialog box. Save your new project. Pick a location on your computer and click **Next**. And we are in! Xcode has pre-populated our project with a basic SpriteKit template.

Navigating our project

Now that we have created our project, you will see the project navigator on the left-hand side of Xcode. You will use the project navigator to add, remove, and rename files and generally organize your project. You might notice that Xcode has created quite a few files in our new project. We will take it slow; don't feel that you have to know what each file does yet, but feel free to explore them if you are curious:

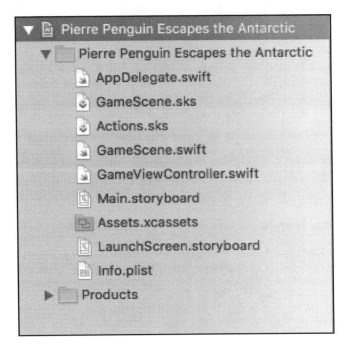

Exploring the SpriteKit demo

Use the project navigator to open up the file named `GameScene.swift`. Xcode created `GameScene.swift` to store the default scene of our new game.

What is a scene? SpriteKit uses the concept of scenes to encapsulate each unique area of a game. Think of the scenes in a movie; we will create a scene for the main menu, a scene for the Game Over screen, a scene for each level in our game, and so on. If you are on the main menu of a game and you tap Play, you move from the menu scene to the Level 1 scene.

 SpriteKit prepends its class names with the letters "SK"; consequently, the scene class is **SKScene**.

You will see there is already some code in this scene. The SpriteKit project template comes with a very small demo. Let's take a quick look at this demo code and use it to test the iOS simulator.

 Please do not be concerned with understanding the demo code at this point. Your focus should be on learning the development environment.

Look for the run toolbar at the top of the Xcode window. It should look something like the following:

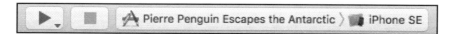

Select the iOS device of your choice to simulate using the dropdown on the far right. Which iOS device should you simulate? You are free to use the device of your choice. I will be using an iPhone SE for the screenshots in this book, so choose **iPhone SE** if you want your results to match my images perfectly.

 Unfortunately, expect your game to play poorly in the simulator. SpriteKit suffers from poor FPS in the iOS simulator. Once our game becomes relatively complex, we will see our FPS drop, even on high-end computers. The simulator will get you through, but it is best if you can plug in a physical device to test.

It is time for our first glimpse of SpriteKit in action! Press the gray play arrow in the toolbar (handy keyboard shortcut: command + r). Xcode will build the project and launch the simulator. The simulator starts in a new window, so make sure you bring it to the front. You should see a gray background with white text: **Hello, World**. Click around on the gray background. You will see colorful, spinning boxes spawning wherever you click:

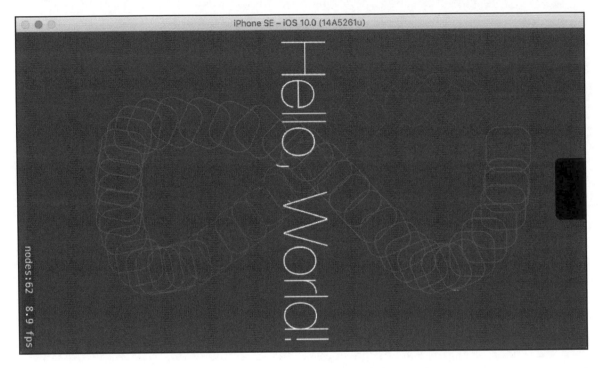

If you have made it this far, congratulations! You have successfully installed and configured everything you need to make your first Swift game.

Once you have finished playing with the spinning squares, you can close the simulator down and return to Xcode. Note: you can use the keyboard command command + q to exit the simulator or press the stop button inside Xcode. If you use the stop button, the simulator will remain open and launch your next build faster.

Examining the demo code

Let's quickly explore the demo code. Do not worry about understanding everything just yet; we will cover each element in depth later. At this point, I am hoping you will acclimatize to the development environment and pick up a few things along the way. If you are stuck, keep going! Things will actually get simpler in the next chapter, once we clear away the SpriteKit demo and start on our own game.

Make sure you have `GameScene.swift` open in Xcode.

The demo `GameScene` class implements some functions you will use in your games. Let's examine these functions. Feel free to read the code inside each function, but I do not expect you to understand the specific code just yet.

- The game invokes the `didMove` function whenever it switches to the `GameScene`. You can think of it a bit like an initialize, or main, function for the scene. The SpriteKit demo uses it to draw the **Hello, World** text to the screen and set up the spinning square shape that shows up when we tap.
- There are seven functions involving touch which handle the user's touch input to the iOS device screen. The SpriteKit demo uses these functions to spawn the spinning square wherever we touch the screen. Do not worry about understanding these functions at this time.
- The `update` function runs once for every frame drawn to the screen. The SpriteKit demo does not use this function, but we may have reason to implement it later.

Cleaning up

I hope that you have absorbed some Swift syntax and gained an overview of Swift and SpriteKit. It is time to make room for our own game; let's clear all of that demo code out! We want to keep a little bit of the boilerplate, but we can delete most of what is inside the functions. To be clear, I do not expect you to understand this code yet. This is simply a necessary step towards the start of our journey.

Firstly, we will remove the **Hello, World** text from the demo. Open the file `GameScene.sks` from the project navigator in Xcode. You will see a gray layout view with **Hello, World** written in the middle. Simply click anywhere on the **Hello, World** text and press your delete key to remove it. Make sure you save your file before moving on.

Secondly, please replace all of the code from your `GameScene.swift` with the following code:

```swift
import SpriteKit

class GameScene: SKScene {
    override func didMove(to view: SKView) {
    }
}
```

Once your `GameScene.swift` looks like the preceding code, you are ready to move on to `Chapter 2`, *Sprites, Camera, Actions!* The real fun begins now!

Summary

You have already accomplished a lot. You have had your first experience with Swift, installed and configured your development environment, launched code successfully into the iOS simulator, and prepared your project for the first steps towards your own game. Great work!

We have seen enough of the "Hello World" demo; are you ready to draw your own graphics to the game screen? We will make use of sprites, textures, colors, and animation in `Chapter 2`, *Sprites, Camera, Action!*

2
Sprites, Camera, Action!

We will start our first game by learning how to draw shapes and textures on the screen. SpriteKit makes drawing simple by doing a lot of the hard work and exposing simple classes we can use for rendering. We are free to focus on building great gameplay experiences while SpriteKit performs the mechanical work of the game loop.

To draw an item on the screen, we create a new instance of a SpriteKit node. These nodes are simple; we attach a child node to our scene, or to existing nodes, for each item we want to draw. Sprites, particle emitters, and text labels are all considered nodes in SpriteKit.

 The **game loop** is a common game design pattern used to constantly update the game many times per second and maintain the same gameplay speed on fast or slow hardware.
SpriteKit wires new nodes into the game loop automatically. As you gain expertise with SpriteKit, you may wish to explore the game loop further to understand what is going on "under the hood".

The topics in this chapter include:

- Preparing your project
- Drawing your first sprite
- Animation: Movement, scaling, and rotation
- Working with textures
- Organizing art into texture atlases
- Centering the camera on a sprite

Sharpening our pencils

There are three quick items to take care of before we start drawing. To begin the preparation, go through the following steps:

1. Since we will design our game to use landscape screen orientations, we will have to disable the portrait view altogether:

    1. With your game project open in Xcode, select the overall project folder in the project navigator (the uppermost item).

    2. You will see your project settings in the main frame of Xcode. Under Deployment Info, find the Device Orientation section.

    3. Uncheck the Portrait option, as shown in the following screenshot:

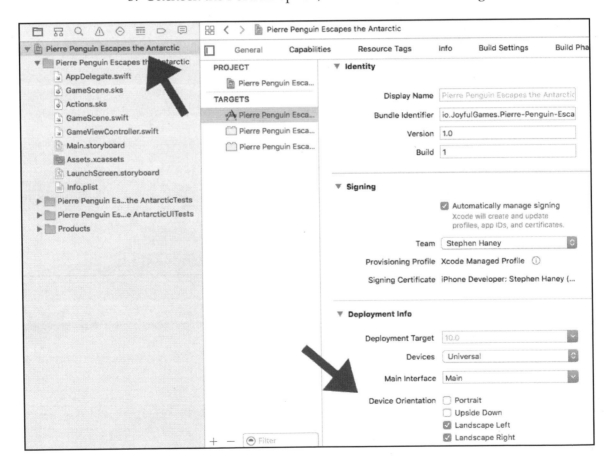

2. We need to resize our scene to fit the new landscape view. Follow these steps to resize the scene:

    1. Open `GameViewController.swift` from the project navigator and locate the `viewDidLoad` function inside the `GameViewController` class. The `viewDidLoad` function is going to fire before the game realizes it is in landscape view, so we need to use a function that fires later in the startup process. Delete `viewDidLoad` completely, removing all of its code.

    2. Replace `viewDidLoad` with a new function named `viewWillLayoutSubviews`. Do not worry about understanding every line right now; we are just configuring our project. Use this code for `viewWillLayoutSubviews`:

```
override func viewWillLayoutSubviews() {
    super.viewWillLayoutSubviews()

    if let view = self.view as! SKView? {
        // Load the SKScene from 'GameScene.sks'
        if let scene = SKScene(fileNamed: "GameScene") {
            // Set the scale mode fit the window:
            scene.scaleMode = .aspectFill
            // Size our scene to fit the view exactly:
            scene.size = view.bounds.size
            // Show the new scene:
            view.presentScene(scene)
        }

        view.ignoresSiblingOrder = true
        view.showsFPS = true
        view.showsNodeCount = true
    }
}
```

    3. Lastly, in `GameViewController.swift`, find the `supportedInterfaceOrientations` function and reduce it to this code:

```
override var supportedInterfaceOrientations:
    UIInterfaceOrientationMask {
    return .landscape
}
```

Downloading the example code

You can download the example code files from your account at
`http://www.packtpub.com` for all the Packt books you have purchased. If
you purchased this book elsewhere, you can visit
`http://www.packtpub.com/support` and register to have the files e-mailed
directly to you.

Additionally, each chapter provides checkpoint links you can use to
download the example project to that point. To get the full list of
checkpoints, visit `http://joyfulgames.io/swift-3-game-development/`

3. We should double-check that we are ready to move on. Try to run our clean
project in the simulator using the toolbar play button or the command + r
keyboard shortcut. After loading, the simulator should switch to landscape view
with a blank gray background (and with the node and FPS counter in the bottom
right). If the project will not run, or you still see "**Hello World**", you will need to
retrace your steps from the end of Chapter 1, *Designing Games with Swift*, namely
the section called *Cleaning Up*, to finish your project preparation.

Checkpoint 2-A

I will provide two checkpoints per chapter, each with a link to download the sample code at
that point in time. I hope this will help you move forward if you are stuck or want to check
your code against mine. If you want to download the sample project upto this point, you
can do so from `http://www.joyfulgames.io/chapter-2`

Drawing your first sprite

It is time to write some game code–fantastic! Open your `GameScene.swift` file and find
the `didMove` function. Recall that this function fires every time the game switches to the
`GameScene`. We will use this function to get familiar with the `SKSpriteNode` class. You
will use `SKSpriteNode` extensively in your game whenever you want to add a new 2D
graphic entity.

The term sprite refers to a 2D graphic or animation that moves around the screen independently from the background. Over time, the term has evolved to refer to any game object on the screen in a 2D game. We will create and draw your first sprite in this chapter: a happy little bee.

Building a SKSpriteNode class

Let's begin by drawing a blue square on the screen. The SKSpriteNode class can draw both texture graphics and solid blocks of color. It is often helpful to prototype your new game ideas with blocks of color before you spend time on artwork. To draw the blue square, add an instance of SKSpriteNode to the game:

```
override func didMove(to view: SKView) {
    // Make the scene position from its lower left
    // corner, regardless of any other settings:
    self.anchorPoint = .zero

    // Instantiate a constant, mySprite, instance of SKSpriteNode
    // The SKSpriteNode constructor can set color and size
    // Note: UIColor is a UIKit class with built-in color presets
    // Note: CGSize is a type we use to set node sizes
    let mySprite = SKSpriteNode(color: .blue, size:
    CGSize(width: 50, height: 50))

    // Assign our sprite a position in points, relative to its
    // parent node (in this case, the scene)
    mySprite.position = CGPoint(x: 150, y: 150)

    // Finally, we need to add our sprite node into the node tree.
    // Call the SKScene'saddChild function to add the node
    // Note: In Swift, 'self' is an automatic property
    // on any type instance, exactly equal to the instance itself
    // So in this case, it refers to the GameScene instance
    self.addChild(mySprite)
}
```

Go ahead and run the project. You should see a similar small blue square appear in your simulator:

Swift allows you to define variables as constants, which can be assigned a value only once. For best performance, use `let` to declare constants whenever possible. Declare your variables with `var` when you need to alter the value later in your code.

Adding animation to your toolkit

Before we dive back in to sprite theory, we should have some fun with our blue square. SpriteKit uses action objects to move sprites around the screen. Consider this example: if our goal is to move the square across the screen, we must first create a new action object to describe the animation. Then, we instruct our sprite node to execute the action. I will illustrate this concept with many examples in the chapter. For now, add this code in the `didMove` function, below the `self.addChild(mySprite)` line:

```
// Create a new constant for our action instance
// Use the move action to provide a goal position for a node
```

```
// SpriteKit will tween to the new position over the course of the
// duration, in this case 5 seconds
let demoAction = SKAction.move(to: CGPoint(x: 300, y: 150),
duration: 3)
// Tell our square node to execute the action!
mySprite.run(demoAction)
```

Run the project. You will see our blue square slide across the screen towards the (300, 150) position. This action is **re-usable**–any node in your scene can execute this action to move to the (300, 150) position. As you can see, SpriteKit does a lot of the heavy lifting for us when we need to animate node properties.

 Inbetweening, or **tweening**, uses the engine to animate smoothly between a start frame and an end frame. Our SKAction.move animation is a tween; we provide the start frame (the sprite's original position) and the end frame (the new destination position). SpriteKit generates the smooth transition between our values.

Let's try some other actions. The SKAction.move function is only one of many options. Try replacing the demoAction line with this code:

```
let demoAction = SKAction.scale(to: 4, duration: 5)
```

Run the project. You will see our blue square grow to four times its original size.

Sequencing multiple animations

We can execute actions together simultaneously, or one after the other, with action groups and sequences. For instance, we can easily make our sprite larger and spin it at the same time. Delete all of our animation code so far and replace it with this code:

```
// Scale up to 4X initial scale
let demoAction1 = SKAction.scale(to: 4, duration: 5)
// Rotate 5 radians
let demoAction2 = SKAction.rotate(byAngle: 5, duration: 5)
// Group the actions
let actionGroup = SKAction.group([demoAction1, demoAction2])
// Execute the group!
mySprite.run(actionGroup)
```

When you run the project, you will see a spinning, growing square. Terrific! If you want to run these actions in sequence (rather than at the same time) change `SKAction.group` to `SKAction.sequence`:

```
// Group the actions into a sequence
let actionSequence = SKAction.sequence([demoAction1, demoAction2])

// Execute the sequence!
mySprite.runAction(actionSequence)
```

Run the code and watch as your square first grows and then spins. Good. We are not limited to two actions; we can group or sequence as many actions together as we need.

We have only used a few actions so far; feel free to explore the `SKAction` class and try out different action combinations before moving on. You can find a full list of actions in Apple's SKAction Class Reference
at: `https://developer.apple.com/library/mac/documentation/SpriteKit/Reference/SKAction_Ref/`

Recapping your first sprite

Congratulations, you have learned to draw a non-textured sprite and animate it with SpriteKit actions. Next, we will explore some important positioning concepts and then add game art to our sprites.

Before you move on, make sure your `didMove` function matches mine and your sequenced animation is firing properly. Here is my code up to this point:

```
override func didMove(to view: SKView) {
    // Make the scene position from its lower left
    // corner, regardless of any other settings:
    self.anchorPoint = .zero

    // Instantiate a constant, mySprite, instance of SKSpriteNode
    let mySprite = SKSpriteNode(color: .blue, size:
        CGSize(width: 50, height: 50))

    // Assign our sprite a position
    mySprite.position = CGPoint(x: 150, y: 150)

    // Add our sprite node into the node tree
    self.addChild(mySprite)

    // Scale up to 4X initial scale
    let demoAction1 = SKAction.scale(to: 4, duration: 5)
```

```
    // Rotate 5 radians
    let demoAction2 = SKAction.rotate(byAngle: 5, duration: 5)

    // Group the actions
    let actionSequence = SKAction.sequence([demoAction1,
        demoAction2])
    // Execute the group!
    mySprite.run(actionSequence)
}
```

The story on positioning

SpriteKit uses a grid of points to position nodes. In this grid, the bottom left corner of the scene is (0,0), with a positive *x*-axis to the right and a positive *y*-axis to the top.

Similarly, on the individual sprite level, (0,0) refers to the bottom left corner of the sprite, while (1,1) refers to the top right corner.

Alignment with anchor points

Each sprite has an anchorPoint property, or an origin. The anchorPoint property allows you to choose which part of the sprite aligns to the sprite's overall position.

The default anchor point is (0.5,0.5), so a new SKSpriteNode centers perfectly on its position.

To illustrate this, let's examine the blue square sprite we just drew on the screen. Our sprite is 50 points wide and 50 points tall, and its position is (150,150). Since we have not modified the `anchorPoint` property, its anchor point is (0.5,0.5). This means the sprite will be perfectly centered over the (150,150) position on the scene's grid. Our sprite's left edge begins at 125 and the right edge terminates at 175. Likewise, the bottom starts at 125 and the top ends at 175. The following diagram illustrates our block's position on the grid:

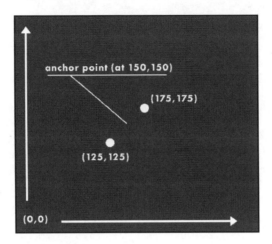

Why do we prefer centered sprites by default? You may think it simpler to position elements by their bottom left corner with an `anchorPoint` property setting of (0,0). However, the centered behavior benefits us when we scale or rotate sprites:

- When we scale a sprite with a bottom left `anchorPoint` property of (0,0), it will only expand up the y-axis and across the x-axis. Rotation actions will swing the sprite in wide circles around its bottom left corner.
- A centered sprite, with the default `anchorPoint` property of (0.5, 0.5), will expand or contract equally in all directions when scaled and will spin in place when rotated, which is usually the desired effect.

There are some cases when you will want to change an anchor point. For instance, if you are drawing a rocket ship, you may want the ship to rotate around the front nose of its cone rather than its center.

Adding textures and game art

You may want to take a screenshot of your blue box for your own enjoyment later. I absolutely love reminiscing over old screenshots of my finished games when they were nothing more than simple colored blocks sliding around the screen. Now it is time to move past that stage and attach some fun artwork to our sprite.

Downloading the free assets

I am providing a downloadable pack for all of the art assets I use in this book. I recommend you use these assets so you will have everything you need for our demo game. Alternatively, you are certainly free to create your own art for your game if you prefer.

These assets come from an outstanding public domain asset pack from *Kenney Game Studio*. I am providing a small subset of the asset pack that we will use in our game. Download the game art from `http://www.joyfulgames.io/assets`

More exceptional art

If you like the art, you can download over 20,000 game assets in the same style for a small donation at `http://kenney.itch.io/kenney-donation`. I do not have an affiliation with Kenney; I just find it admirable that he has released so much public domain artwork for indie game developers.

These assets are public domain, which means you can copy, modify, and distribute the art, even for commercial purposes, all without asking permission. You can read the full license at `https://creativecommons.org/publicdomain/zero/1.0/`

Drawing your first textured sprite

Let's use some of the graphics you just downloaded. We will start by creating a bee sprite. We will add the bee texture to our project, load the image onto a `SKSpriteNode` class, and then size the node for optimum sharpness on retina screens.

Adding the bee image to your project

We need to add the image files to our Xcode project before we can use them in the game. Once we add the images, we can reference them by name in our code; SpriteKit is smart enough to find and implement the graphics. Follow these steps to add the bee image to the project:

1. Right-click on your project in the project navigator and click **Add Files to "Pierre Penguin Escapes the Antarctic"** (or the name of your game). Refer to this screenshot to find the correct menu item:

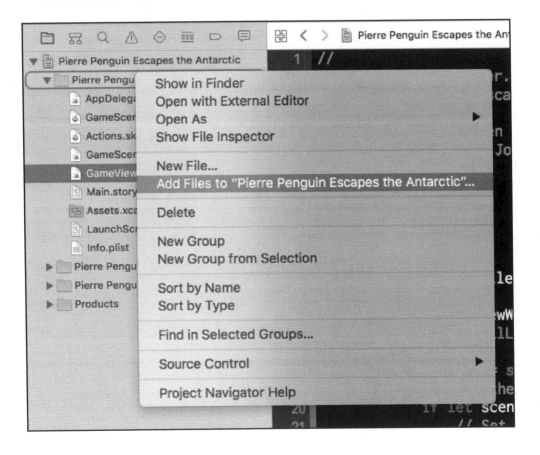

2. Browse to the asset pack you downloaded and locate the bee@3x.png image inside the Enemies folder.
3. Check **Copy items if needed**, then click **Add**.

You should now see bee@3x.png in your project navigator.

Loading images with SKSpriteNode

It is quite easy to draw images to the screen with SKSpriteNode. Start by clearing out all of the code we wrote for the blue square inside the didMove function in GameScene.swift. Replace didMove with this code:

```
override func didMove(to view: SKView) {
    // Position from the lower left corner
    self.anchorPoint = .zero
    // set the scene's background to a nice sky blue
    // Note: UIColor uses a scale from 0 to 1 for its colors
    self.backgroundColor = UIColor(red: 0.4, green: 0.6, blue:
    0.95, alpha: 1.0)

    // create our bee sprite node
    let bee = SKSpriteNode(imageNamed: "bee")
    // size our bee node
    bee.size = CGSize(width: 100, height: 100)
    // position our bee node
    bee.position = CGPoint(x: 250, y: 250)
    // attach our bee to the scene's node tree
    self.addChild(bee)
}
```

Run the project and witness our glorious bee–great work!

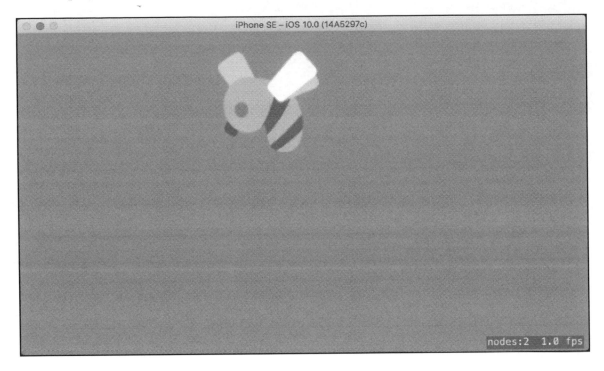

Designing for retina

You may notice that our bee image is quite blurry. To take advantage of retina screens, assets need to be twice the pixel dimensions of their node's size property (for most retina screens), or three times the node size for the Plus versions of the iPhone. Ignore the height for a moment; our bee node is 100 points wide, but the PNG file is only 84 pixels wide. The PNG file needs to be 300 pixels wide to look sharp on the Plus-sized iPhones, or 200 pixels wide to look sharp on 2X retina devices.

SpriteKit will automatically resize textures to fit their nodes, so one approach is to create a giant texture at the highest retina resolution (three times the node size) and let SpriteKit resize the texture down for lower density screens. However, there is a considerable performance penalty, and older devices can even run out of memory and crash from the huge textures.

The ideal asset approach

These double and triple-sized retina assets can be confusing to new iOS developers. To solve this issue, Xcode lets you provide three image files for each texture. For example, our bee node is currently 100 points wide and 100 points tall. You can provide the following images to Xcode and it will automatically use the image best suited to the device.

- Bee.png (100 pixels by 100 pixels)
- Bee@2x.png (200 pixels by 200 pixels)
- Bee@3x.png (300 pixels by 300 pixels)

Simplifying matters, Swift only runs on iOS7 and higher. The only non-retina devices that run iOS7 are the aging iPad 2 and iPad Mini 1st generation. If these older devices are important for your finished games, you should create all three sizes of images for your games. Otherwise, you can safely ignore non-retina assets with Swift and create only 2X and 3X sized images.

Hands-on with retina in SpriteKit

Our bee image illustrates how this all works:

- Because we set an explicit node size, SpriteKit automatically resizes the bee texture to fit our 100 point wide, 100 point tall node. This automatic size-to-fit is very handy, but notice that we have actually slightly distorted the aspect ratio of the image.
- If we do not set an explicit size, SpriteKit sizes the node to match the texture's dimensions. Go ahead and delete the line that sets the size for our bee node and rerun the project. SpriteKit maintains the aspect ratio automatically and sizes the bee correctly down to 28 points by 24 points based on the @3x suffix.
- This works wonderfully, but I still like to set my node sizes explicitly. Set the size property of your bee node to 28 points wide by 24 points tall:

```
// size our bee in points:
bee.size = CGSize(width: 28, height: 24)
```

Run the project and you will see a smaller, crystal sharp bee, as in this screenshot:

Great! The important concept here is to design your art files at three times the point sizes of your sprite nodes to take full advantage of 3x retina screens. Now we will look at organizing and animating multiple sprite frames.

Organizing your assets

We will quickly overrun our project navigator with image files if we add all our textures as we did with our bee. Luckily, Xcode provides several solutions.

Exploring Assets.xcassets

We can store images in an `.xcassets` file and refer to them easily from our code. Follow these steps to prepare our `.xcassets` file:

1. Open `Assets.xcassets` from your project navigator.
2. Notice that SpriteKit placed a demo spaceship image here. We do not need it, so we can right-click on it and choose **Remove Selected Items** to delete it.
3. You will also see an empty **AppIcon** entry. You can leave it there for now; we will revisit the AppIcon later.

Collecting art into texture atlases

We will use texture atlases for most of our in-game art. Texture atlases organize assets by collecting related artwork together. They also increase performance by optimizing all of the images inside each atlas as if they were one texture. SpriteKit only needs one draw call to render multiple images out of the same texture atlas. Plus, they are very easy to use! Follow these steps to build your bee texture atlas:

1. First, we need to remove our old bee texture. Right-click on `bee@3x.png` in the project navigator and choose **Delete**, then **Move to Trash**.
2. In `Assets.xcassets`, right-click in the left panel and select **New Sprite Atlas**.
3. You should see a new folder in the left panel called **Sprites**. This is our new texture atlas. Double-click it, or select it, and press your enter key to rename it, then name it as **Enemies** (the bee will eventually be an enemy in our game).
4. Inside this atlas, you will see a demo entry called **Sprite**. We can delete this demo sprite; we will create our own entries for our game. Right-click **Sprite** and select `Remove Selected Items`.
5. Open the asset bundle that you downloaded and locate the `bee@2x.png` and `bee@3x.png` images inside the `Enemies` folder.

6. There are several ways to import files into a texture atlas. The easiest is to select all sizes of the image in the Finder and then drag and drop them onto the **Enemies** texture atlas icon in the left panel of Xcode. You can do this now, and you should see a new sprite created inside **Enemies** called **bee**, as shown in this screenshot:

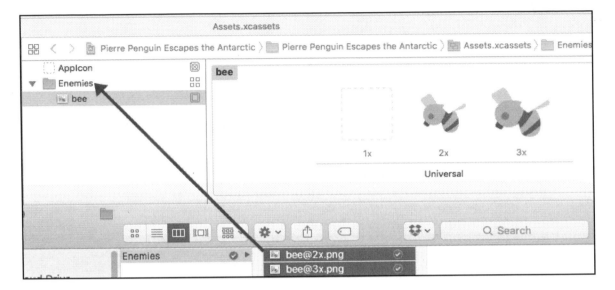

7. We also want to create another sprite in this atlas for the second frame of our bee's flying animation. Repeat this drag and drop exercise by selecting the asset files named `bee-fly@2x.png` and `bee-fly@3x.png` and dragging them onto the **Enemies** texture atlas in Xcode.

You should now have a texture atlas named **Enemies** that contains two sprites: **bee** and **bee-fly**. Each of these sprites has both a 2X and 3X version to take full advantage of retina screens. Good work; we have organized our bee assets into one collection. Xcode will now automatically create performance optimizations and select the best size for each device.

Updating our bee node to use the texture atlas

We can actually run our project right now and see the same bee as before. Our old bee texture was `bee`, and a new `bee` sprite exists in the texture atlas. Although we deleted the standalone `bee@3x.png`, SpriteKit is smart enough to find the new `bee` in the texture atlas.

We should make sure our texture atlas is working and that we successfully deleted the old individual `bee@3x.png`. In `GameScene.swift`, change our `SKSpriteNode` instantiation line to use the new `bee-fly` graphic from the texture atlas:

```
// create our bee sprite
// notice the new image name: bee-fly
let bee = SKSpriteNode(imageNamed: "bee-fly")
```

Run the project again. You should see a different bee image, its wings held lower than before. This is the second frame of the bee animation. Next, we will learn to animate between the two frames to create an animated sprite.

Iterating through texture atlas frames

We need to study one more texture atlas technique: we can quickly flip through multiple sprite frames to make our bee come alive with motion. We now have two frames of our bee in flight; it should appear to hover in place if we switch back and forth between these frames.

Our node will run a new `SKAction` to animate between the two frames. Update your `didMove` function to match mine (I removed some older comments to save space):

```
override func didMove(to view: SKView) {
    self.anchorPoint = .zero
    self.backgroundColor = UIColor(red: 0.4, green: 0.6, blue:
        0.95, alpha: 1.0)

    // create our bee sprite
    // Note: Remove all prior arguments from this line:
    let bee = SKSpriteNode()
    bee.position = CGPoint(x: 250, y: 250)
    bee.size = CGSize(width: 28, height: 24)
    self.addChild(bee)

    // Find our new bee texture atlas
    let beeAtlas = SKTextureAtlas(named:"Enemies")
    // Grab the two bee frames from the texture atlas in an array
    // Note: Check out the syntax explicitly declaring beeFrames
    // as an array of SKTextures. This is not strictly necessary,
    // but it makes the intent of the code more readable, so I
    // chose to include the explicit type declaration here:
    let beeFrames:[SKTexture] = [
        beeAtlas.textureNamed("bee"),
        beeAtlas.textureNamed("bee-fly")]
    // Create a new SKAction to animate between the frames once
```

```
    let flyAction = SKAction.animate(with: beeFrames,
        timePerFrame: 0.14)
    // Create an SKAction to run the flyAction repeatedly
    let beeAction = SKAction.repeatForever(flyAction)
    // Instruct our bee to run the final repeat action:
    bee.run(beeAction)
}
```

Run the project. You will see our bee flap its wings back and forth–cool! You have learned the basics of sprite animation with texture atlases. We will create increasingly complicated animations using this same technique later in the book. For now, pat yourself on the back. The result may seem simple, but you have unlocked a major building block towards your first SpriteKit game!

Putting it all together

First, we learned how to use actions to move, scale, and rotate our sprites. Then, we explored animating through multiple frames, bringing our sprite to life. Let's now combine these techniques to fly our bee back and forth across the screen, flipping the texture at each turn.

Add this code at the bottom of the `didMove` function, beneath the `bee.run(beeAction)` line:

```
// Set up new actions to move our bee back and forth:
let pathLeft = SKAction.moveBy(x: -200, y: -10, duration: 2)
let pathRight = SKAction.moveBy(x: 200, y: 10, duration: 2)
// These two scaleX actions flip the texture back and forth
// We will use these to turn the bee to face left and right
let flipTextureNegative = SKAction.scaleX(to: -1, duration: 0)
let flipTexturePositive = SKAction.scaleX(to: 1, duration: 0)
// Combine actions into a cohesive flight sequence for our bee
let flightOfTheBee = SKAction.sequence([pathLeft,
flipTextureNegative, pathRight, flipTexturePositive])
// Last, create a looping action that will repeat forever
let neverEndingFlight =
    SKAction.repeatForever(flightOfTheBee)

// Tell our bee to run the flight path, and away it goes!
bee.run(neverEndingFlight)
```

Run the project. You will see the bee flying back and forth, flapping its wings. You have officially learned the fundamentals of animation in SpriteKit! We will build on this knowledge to create a rich, animated game world for our players.

Centering the camera on a sprite

Games often require that the camera follows the player sprite as it moves through space. We definitely want this camera behavior for Pierre, our penguin character, whom we will soon be adding to the game. With iOS9, Apple added a new SKCameraNode class that makes this task easy. We will attach a SKCameraNode to our scene and position it directly over the player to keep their character centered in the view.

You can find the code for our camera functionality in the following code block. Read the comments for a detailed explanation. This is a quick recap of the changes:

- Our didMove function was becoming too crowded. I broke out our flying bee code into a new function named addTheFlyingBee. Later, we will encapsulate game objects, such as bees, into their own classes.
- I created two new constants on the GameScene class: the camera node and the bee node.
- I updated the didMove function. It assigns the new camera node to the scene's camera.
- Inside the new addTheFlyingBee function, I removed the bee constant, as GameScene now declares it above as its own property.
- We are implementing a new function: didSimulatePhysics. SpriteKit calls this function every frame, after performing physics calculations and adjusting positions. It's a great place to update our camera position. The code to change the camera position and keep the view centered on the player resides in this new function.

Please update your entire GameScene.swift file to match mine:

```swift
import SpriteKit

class GameScene: SKScene {
    // Create a constant cam as a SKCameraNode:
    let cam = SKCameraNode()
    // Create our bee node as a property of GameScene so we can
    // access it throughout the class
    // (Make sure to remove the old bee declaration below)
    let bee = SKSpriteNode()

    override func didMove(to view: SKView) {
        self.anchorPoint = .zero
        self.backgroundColor = UIColor(red: 0.4, green: 0.6, blue:
            0.95, alpha: 1.0)
```

```
        // Assign the camera to the scene
        self.camera = cam

        // Call the new bee function
        self.addTheFlyingBee()
    }

    // A new function
    override func didSimulatePhysics() {
        // Keep the camera centered on the bee
        // Notice the ! operator after camera. SKScene's camera
        // is an optional, but we know it is there since we
        // assigned it above in the didMove function. We can tell
        // Swift that we know it can unwrap this value by using
        // the ! operator after the property name.
        self.camera!.position = bee.position
    }

    // I moved all of our bee animation code into a new function:
    func addTheFlyingBee() {
        // Position our bee
        bee.position = CGPoint(x: 250, y: 250)
        bee.size = CGSize(width: 28, height: 24)
        // Add the bee to the scene
        self.addChild(bee)

        // Find the bee textures from the texture atlas
        let beeAtlas = SKTextureAtlas(named:"Enemies")
        let beeFrames:[SKTexture] = [
            beeAtlas.textureNamed("bee"),
            beeAtlas.textureNamed("bee-fly")]
        // Create a new SKAction to animate between the frames
        let flyAction = SKAction.animate(with: beeFrames,
            timePerFrame: 0.14)
        // Create an SKAction to run the flyAction repeatedly
        let beeAction = SKAction.repeatForever(flyAction)
        // Instruct our bee to run the final repeat action:
            bee.run(beeAction)

        // Set up new actions to move our bee back and forth:
        let pathLeft =
            SKAction.moveBy(x: -200, y: -10, duration: 2)
        let pathRight =
            SKAction.moveBy(x: 200, y: 10, duration: 2)
        let flipTextureNegative =
            SKAction.scaleX(to: -1, duration: 0)
        let flipTexturePositive =
            SKAction.scaleX(to: 1, duration: 0)
```

```
    // Combine actions into a cohesive flight sequence
    let flightOfTheBee = SKAction.sequence([
        pathLeft,flipTextureNegative, pathRight,
            flipTexturePositive])
    // Last, create a looping action that will repeat forever
    let neverEndingFlight =
        SKAction.repeatForever(flightOfTheBee)

    // Tell our bee to run the flight path, and away it goes!
    bee.run(neverEndingFlight)
    }
}
```

Run the game. You should see our bee stuck directly at the center of the screen, flipping back and forth every two seconds.

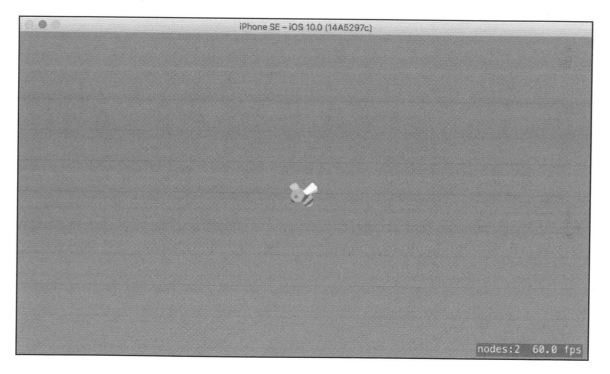

The bee is actually changing position, just as before, but the camera is moving to keep the bee centered on the screen. When we add more game objects in Chapter 3, *Mix in the Physics*, our bee will appear to fly as the entire world pans past the screen.

Checkpoint 2-B

We have made many changes to our project in this chapter. If you would like to download my project upto this point, do so at `http://www.joyfulgames.io/chapter-2`

Summary

You have gained foundational knowledge of sprites, nodes, and actions in SpriteKit, and have already taken huge strides towards your first game with Swift.

You configured your project for landscape orientation, drew your first sprite, and then made it move, spin, and scale. You added a bee texture to your sprite, created an image atlas, and animated through the frames of flight. Lastly, you built a camera to keep the gameplay centered on the player. Terrific work!

In the next chapter, we will use SpriteKit's physics engine to assign weight and gravity to our world, spawn more flying characters, and create the ground and sky.

3
Mix in the Physics

SpriteKit includes a fully functional physics engine. It is easy to implement and very useful, as most mobile game designs require some level of physical interaction between game objects. In our game, we want to know when the player runs into the ground, an enemy, or a power-up. The physics system can track these collisions and execute our specific game code when any of these events occur. SpriteKit's physics engine can also apply gravity to the world–as well as the bounce and spin that can occur when sprites collide with each other–and creates realistic movement through impulses; and it does all of this before every single frame is drawn on the screen!

The topics in this chapter include the following:

- Adopting a protocol for consistency
- Organizing game objects into classes
- Adding the player's character
- Renovating the GameScene class
- Physics bodies and gravity
- Exploring physics simulation mechanics
- Movement with impulses and forces
- Bumping bees into bees

Laying the foundation

So far, we have learned through small bits of code, individually added to the `GameScene` class. The intricacy of our application is about to increase. To build a complex game world, we will need to construct re-usable classes and actively organize our new code.

Following protocol

To start, we want individual classes for each of our game objects (a bee class, a player penguin class, a power-up class, and so on). Furthermore, we want all of our game object classes to share a consistent set of properties and methods. We can enforce this commonality by creating a **protocol**, or a blueprint, for our game classes. The protocol does not provide any functionality on its own, but each class that adopts the protocol must follow its specifications exactly before Xcode can compile the project. Protocols are very similar to interfaces, if you are from a Java or C# background.

Add a new file to your project (right-click in the project navigator and choose **New File**, then **Swift File**) and name it GameSprite.swift. Then, add the following code to your new file:

```
import SpriteKit

protocol GameSprite {
    var textureAtlas:SKTextureAtlas { get set }
    var initialSize: CGSize { get set }
    func onTap()
}
```

Now, any class that adopts the GameSprite protocol must implement a textureAtlas property, an initialSize property, and an onTap function. We can safely assume that the game objects provide these implementations when we work with them in our code.

Reinventing the bee

Our old bee is working wonderfully, but we want to spawn many bees throughout the world. We will create a Bee class, inheriting from SKSpriteNode, so we can cleanly stamp as many bees to the world as we please.

It is a common convention to separate each class into its own file. Add a new Swift file to your project and name it Bee.swift. Then, add the following code:

```
import SpriteKit

// Create the new class Bee, inheriting from SKSpriteNode
// and adopting the GameSprite protocol:
class Bee: SKSpriteNode, GameSprite {
    // We will store our size, texture atlas, and animations
    // as class wide properties.
    var initialSize:CGSize = CGSize(width: 28, height: 24)
    var textureAtlas:SKTextureAtlas =
```

```
            SKTextureAtlas(named:"Enemies")
        var flyAnimation = SKAction()

        // The init function will be called when Bee is instantiated:
        init() {
            // Call the init function on the base class (SKSpriteNode)
            // We pass nil for the texture since we will animate the
            // texture ourselves.
            super.init(texture: nil, color: .clear, size:
                initialSize)
            // Create and run the flying animation:
            createAnimations()
            self.run(flyAnimation)
        }

        // Our bee only implements one texture based animation.
        // But some classes may be more complicated,
        // So we break out the animation building into this function:
        func createAnimations() {
            let flyFrames:[SKTexture] =
                [textureAtlas.textureNamed("bee"),
                textureAtlas.textureNamed("bee-fly")]
            let flyAction = SKAction.animate(with: flyFrames,
                timePerFrame: 0.14)
            flyAnimation = SKAction.repeatForever(flyAction)
        }

        // onTap is not wired up yet, but we have to implement this
        // function to conform to our GameSprite protocol.
        // We will explore touch events in the next chapter.
        func onTap() {}

        // Lastly, we are required to add this bit of boilerplate
        // to subclass SKSpriteNode. We will need to do this any
        // time we inherit from SKSpriteNode and use an init function
        required init?(coder aDecoder: NSCoder) {
            super.init(coder: aDecoder)
        }
    }
```

It is now easy to spawn as many bees as we like. Switch back to GameScene.swift and add this code at the bottom of didMove:

```
// Add a second Bee to the scene:
let bee2 = Bee()
bee2.position = CGPoint(x: 325, y: 325)
self.addChild(bee2)
// ... and a third Bee:
```

```
let bee3 = Bee()
bee3.position = CGPoint(x: 200, y: 325)
self.addChild(bee3)
```

Run the project **Bees, bees everywhere!** Our original bee is flying back and forth through a swarm. Your simulator should look like this:

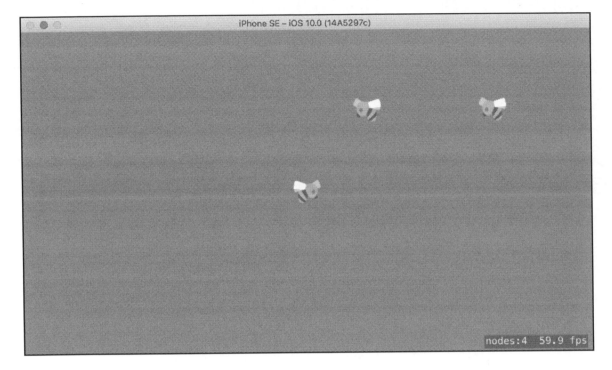

Depending on how you look at it, you may perceive that the new bees are moving and the original bee is still. We need to add a point of reference; next, we will add the ground.

The icy tundra

We will add some ground at the bottom of the screen to serve as a constraint for player positioning and as a reference point for movement. We will need to create a new class named Ground. First, let's add the texture atlas for the ground art to our project.

Adding the ground texture to Assets.xcassets

We need to add our ground texture sprite, just as we added the bee sprites earlier. Once again, we will create a texture atlas in the `Assets.xcassets` file to hold our ground texture and other environmental textures we will use along the way. Follow these steps to add the ground texture to our project:

1. Open the `Assets.xcassets` file in Xcode, then right-click in the left panel and select **New Sprite Atlas**.

2. Change the name of the new sprite atlas from **Sprites** to **Environment** (we will use this texture atlas for all the environment textures in our game).

3. Xcode creates a new sprite–named **Sprite**–inside this atlas by default. Remove it by right-clicking it and selecting **Remove Selected Items**.

4. In Finder, open the asset pack you downloaded. Locate the **Environment** folder and select `ground@2x.png` and `ground@3x.png`.

5. Drag and drop these two files into Xcode on top of the **Environment** texture atlas.

Xcode should create a new sprite named **ground** inside the **Environment** atlas. When you are done, your `Assets.xcassets` should look like this:

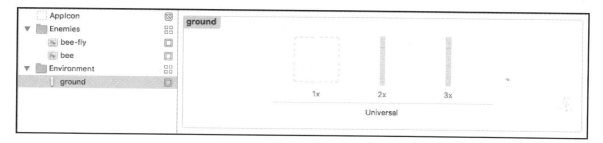

Adding the Ground class

Next, we will add the code for the ground. Add a new Swift file to your project and name it `Ground.swift`. Use the following code:

```
import SpriteKit

// A new class, inheriting from SKSpriteNode and
// adhering to the GameSprite protocol.
class Ground: SKSpriteNode, GameSprite {
    var textureAtlas:SKTextureAtlas =
        SKTextureAtlas(named: "Environment")
    // We will not use initialSize for ground, but we still need
```

```
    // to declare it to conform to our GameSprite protocol:
    var initialSize = CGSize.zero

    // This function tiles the ground texture across the width
    // of the Ground node. We will call it from our GameScene.
    func createChildren() {
        // This is one of those unique situations where we use a
        // non-default anchor point. By positioning the ground by
        // its top left corner, we can place it just slightly
        // above the bottom of the screen, on any of screen size.
        self.anchorPoint = CGPoint(x: 0, y: 1)

        // First, load the ground texture from the atlas:
        let texture = textureAtlas.textureNamed("ground")

        var tileCount:CGFloat = 0
        // We will size the tiles in their point size
        // They are 35 points wide and 300 points tall
        let tileSize = CGSize(width: 35, height: 300)

        // Build nodes until we cover the entire Ground width
        while tileCount * tileSize.width < self.size.width {
            let tileNode = SKSpriteNode(texture: texture)
            tileNode.size = tileSize
            tileNode.position.x = tileCount * tileSize.width
            // Position child nodes by their upper left corner
            tileNode.anchorPoint = CGPoint(x: 0, y: 1)
            // Add the child texture to the ground node:
            self.addChild(tileNode)

            tileCount += 1
        }
    }

    // Implement onTap to adhere to the protocol:
    func onTap() {}
}
```

Tiling a texture

Why do we need the `createChildren` function? This is one method of tiling textures. We can create a child node for each texture tile and append them across the width of the parent. Performance is not an issue; as long as we attach the children to one parent, and the textures all come from the same texture atlas, SpriteKit handles them with one draw call.

Running wire to the ground

We have added the ground art to the project and created the Ground class. The final step is to create an instance of Ground in our scene. Follow these steps to wire up the ground:

1. Open `GameScene.swift` and add a new property to the `GameScene` class to create an instance of the Ground class. You can place this underneath the line that instantiates the `cam` node (the new code is in bold):

   ```
   let cam = SKCameraNode()
   let ground = Ground()
   ```

2. Locate the `didMove` function. Add the following code at the bottom, underneath our bee-spawning lines:

   ```
   // Position the ground based on the screen size.
   // Position X: Negative one screen width.
   // Position Y: 150 above the bottom (remember the top
   // left anchor point).
   ground.position = CGPoint(x: -self.size.width * 2, y: 150)
   // Set the ground width to 3x the width of the scene
   // The height can be 0, our child nodes will create the height
   ground.size = CGSize(width: self.size.width * 6, height: 0)
   // Run the ground's createChildren function to build
   // the child texture tiles:
   ground.createChildren()
   // Add the ground node to the scene:
   self.addChild(ground)
   ```

Run the project. You will see the icy tundra appear underneath our bees. This small change goes a long way toward creating the feeling that our central bee is moving through space. Your simulator should look like this:

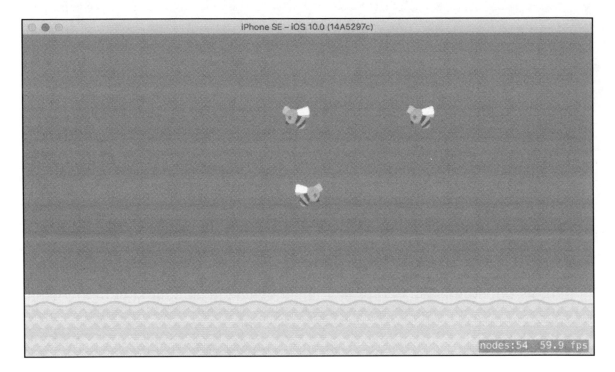

A wild penguin appears!

There is one more class to build before we start our physics lesson: The `Player` class! It is time to replace our moving bee with a node designated as the player.

First, we will add the sprite atlas for our penguin art. By now, you are familiar with adding new sprite atlases and sprites to the `Assets.xcassets` file. Follow these steps to add the flying penguin art to your project:

1. Create a new sprite atlas named `Pierre` in `Assets.xcassets` by right-clicking in the left panel and selecting **New Sprite Atlas**.
2. Locate the `Pierre` folder in your downloaded asset bundle. Drag and drop all of the `.png` files from this folder onto the `Pierre` atlas in Xcode.

3. Your `Assets.xcassets` file should now look like this:

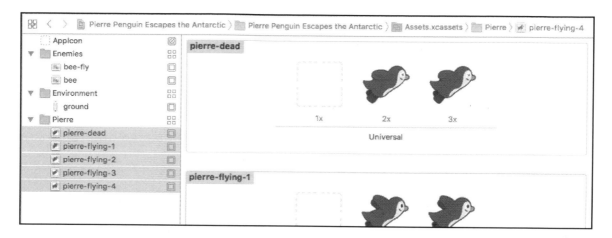

4. Now that you have Pierre Penguin's textures in a texture atlas, you can create the `Player` class. Add a new Swift file to your project and name it `Player.swift`. Then, add this code:

```
import SpriteKit

class Player : SKSpriteNode, GameSprite {
    var initialSize = CGSize(width: 64, height: 64)
    var textureAtlas:SKTextureAtlas =
        SKTextureAtlas(named:"Pierre")
    // Pierre has multiple animations. Right now, we will
    // create one animation for flying up,
    // and one for going down:
    var flyAnimation = SKAction()
    var soarAnimation = SKAction()

    init() {
        // Call the init function on the
        // base class (SKSpriteNode)
        super.init(texture: nil, color: .clear, size:
                initialSize)

        createAnimations()
        // If we run an action with a key, "flapAnimation",
        // we can later reference that
        // key to remove the action.
        self.run(flyAnimation, withKey: "flapAnimation")
    }
```

```swift
func createAnimations() {
    let rotateUpAction =
    SKAction.rotate(toAngle: 0, duration: 0.475)
    rotateUpAction.timingMode = .easeOut
    let rotateDownAction = SKAction.rotate(toAngle: -1,
        duration: 0.8)
    rotateDownAction.timingMode = .easeIn

    // Create the flying animation:
    let flyFrames:[SKTexture] = [
        textureAtlas.textureNamed("pierre-flying-1"),
        textureAtlas.textureNamed("pierre-flying-2"),
        textureAtlas.textureNamed("pierre-flying-3"),
        textureAtlas.textureNamed("pierre-flying-4"),
        textureAtlas.textureNamed("pierre-flying-3"),
        textureAtlas.textureNamed("pierre-flying-2")
    ]
    let flyAction = SKAction.animate(with: flyFrames,
        timePerFrame: 0.03)
    // Group together the flying animation with rotation:
    flyAnimation = SKAction.group([
        SKAction.repeatForever(flyAction),
        rotateUpAction
    ])

    // Create the soaring animation,
    // just one frame for now:
    let soarFrames:[SKTexture] =
    [textureAtlas.textureNamed("pierre-flying-1")]
    let soarAction = SKAction.animate(with: soarFrames,
        timePerFrame: 1)
    // Group the soaring animation with the rotation down:
    soarAnimation = SKAction.group([
        SKAction.repeatForever(soarAction),
        rotateDownAction
    ])
}

// Implement onTap to conform to the GameSprite protocol:
func onTap() {}

// Satisfy the NSCoder required init:
required init?(coder aDecoder: NSCoder) {
    super.init(coder: aDecoder)
}
}
```

Great! Before we continue, we need to replace our original bee with an instance of the new Player class we just created. Follow these steps to replace the bee:

1. In GameScene.swift, near the top, remove the line that creates a bee constant in the GameScene class. Instead, we want to initiate an instance of Player. Add the new line let player = Player().

2. Completely delete the addTheFlyingBee function.

3. In didMove, remove the line that calls addTheFlyingBee.

4. In didMove, at the bottom, add new code to position and add the player:

```
// Position the player:
player.position = CGPoint(x: 150, y: 250)
// Add the player node to the scene:
self.addChild(player)
```

5. Further down, in didSimulatePhysics, replace the reference to the bee with a reference to the player. The new line will read: self.camera!.position = **player**.position. Recall that we created the didSimulatePhysics function in Chapter 2, *Sprites, Camera, Actions!* when we centered the camera on one node.

We have successfully transformed the original bee into a penguin. Before we move on, we will make sure your GameScene class includes all of the changes we have made so far in this chapter. After that, we will begin to explore the physics system.

Renovating the GameScene class

We have made quite a few changes to our project. Luckily, this is the last major overhaul of the previous animation code. Moving forward, we will use the terrific structure we built in this chapter. At this point, your GameScene.swift file should look something like the following:

```
import SpriteKit

class GameScene: SKScene {
    let cam = SKCameraNode()
    let ground = Ground()
    let player = Player()

    override func didMove(to view: SKView) {
        self.anchorPoint = .zero
        self.backgroundColor = UIColor(red: 0.4, green: 0.6, blue:
            0.95, alpha: 1.0)
```

```
        // Assign the camera to the scene
        self.camera = cam

        // Spawn our test bees:
        let bee2 = Bee()
        bee2.position = CGPoint(x: 325, y: 325)
        self.addChild(bee2)
        let bee3 = Bee()
        bee3.position = CGPoint(x: 200, y: 325)
        self.addChild(bee3)

        // Add the ground to the scene:
        ground.position = CGPoint(x: -self.size.width * 2, y: 150)
        ground.size = CGSize(width: self.size.width * 6,
                height: 0)
        ground.createChildren()
        self.addChild(ground)

        // Add the player to the scene:
        player.position = CGPoint(x: 150, y: 250)
        self.addChild(player)
    }

    override func didSimulatePhysics() {
        // Keep the camera centered on the player
        self.camera!.position = player.position
    }
}
```

Run the project. You will see our new penguin hovering near the bees. Great work; we are now ready to explore the physics system with all of our new nodes. Your simulator should look something like this screenshot:

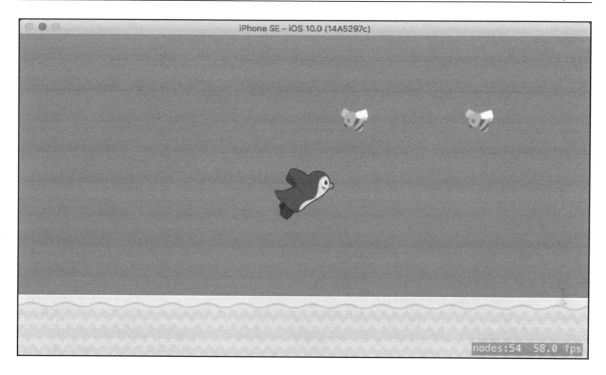

Exploring the physics system

SpriteKit simulates physics with physics bodies. We attach physics bodies to all the nodes that need physics computations. We will set up a quick example before exploring all of the details.

Dropping like flies

Our bees need to be part of the physics simulation, so we will add physics bodies to their nodes. Open your Bee.swift file and locate the init function. Add the following code at the bottom of the function:

```
// Attach a physics body, shaped like a circle
// and sized roughly to our bee.
self.physicsBody = SKPhysicsBody(circleOfRadius: size.width / 2)
```

It is that easy to add a node to the physics simulation. Run the project. You will see our two bee instances drop off the screen. They are now subject to gravity, which is on by default.

Solidifying the ground

We want the ground to catch falling game objects. We can give the ground its own physics body so that the physics simulation can stop the bees from falling through it. Open your `Ground.swift` file, locate the `createChildren` function, and add this code at the bottom of the function:

```
// Draw an edge physics body along the top of the ground node.
// Note: physics body positions are relative to their nodes.
// The top left of the node is X: 0, Y: 0, given our anchor point.
// The top right of the node is X: size.width, Y: 0
let pointTopLeft = CGPoint(x: 0, y: 0)
let pointTopRight = CGPoint(x: size.width, y: 0)
self.physicsBody = SKPhysicsBody(edgeFrom: pointTopLeft,
    to: pointTopRight)
```

Run the project. The bees will now quickly drop and then stop once they collide with the ground. After the bees have landed, your simulator will look like the following:

Checkpoint 3-A

Great work so far. We have added a lot of structure to our game, and have started to explore the physics system. If you would like to download my project up to this point, you can do so at `http://www.joyfulgames.io/chapter-3`.

Exploring physics simulation mechanics

Let's take a closer look at the specifics of SpriteKit's physics system. For instance, why are the bees subject to gravity while the ground stays where it is? Though we attached physics bodies to both nodes, we actually used two different styles of physics bodies. There are three types of physics bodies, and each behaves slightly differently:

- **Dynamic:** Physics bodies have volume and are fully subject to forces and collisions in the system. We will use dynamic physics bodies for most parts of the game world: the player, enemies, power-ups, and others.
- **Static:** Physics bodies have volume but no velocity. The physics simulation does not move nodes with static bodies, but they can still collide with other game objects. We can use static bodies for walls or obstacles.
- **Edge:** Physics bodies have no volume and the physics simulation will never move them. They mark off the boundaries of movement; other physics bodies will never cross them. Edges can cross each other to create small containment areas.

Voluminous (dynamic and static) bodies have a variety of properties that influence how they move through space and react to collisions. This allows us to create a wide range of realistic physics effects. Each property controls one aspect of a body's physical characteristics:

- **Restitution:** Determines how much energy is lost when one body bounces into another. This changes the body's bounciness. SpriteKit measures restitution on a scale from 0.0 to 1.0. The default value is 0.2.
- **Friction:** Describes the amount of force necessary to slide one body against another body. This property also uses a scale of 0.0 to 1.0, with a default value of 0.2.
- **Damping:** Determines how quickly a body slows as it moves through space. You can think of damping as air friction. Linear damping determines how quickly a body loses speed, while angular damping affects rotation. Both measure from 0.0 to 1.0, with a default value of 0.1.

- **Mass:** Measured in kilograms. It describes how far colliding objects push the body and factors in momentum during movement. Bodies with more mass will move less when hit by another body and will push other bodies further when they collide with them. The physics engine automatically uses the mass and the area of the body to determine **density**. Alternatively, you can set the density and let the physics engine calculate mass. It is usually more intuitive to set the mass.

All right, enough with the textbook! Let's solidify our learning with some examples.

Firstly, we want gravity to leave our bees alone. We will set their flight paths manually. We need the bees to be dynamic physics bodies in order to interact properly with other nodes, but we need these bodies to ignore gravity. For such instances, SpriteKit provides a property named `affectedByGravity`. Open `Bee.swift` and, at the bottom of the `init` function, add this code:

```
self.physicsBody?.affectedByGravity = false
```

The question mark after `physics Body` is optional chaining. We need to unwrap `physicsBody`, since it is optional. If `physicsBody` is nil, the entire statement will return nil (instead of triggering an error). You can think of it as gracefully unwrapping an optional property with an inline statement.

Run the project. The bees should now hover in place, as they did before we added their bodies, however, SpriteKit's physics simulation now affects them; they will react to impulses and collisions. Great–let's purposefully collide the bees.

Bee meets bee

You may have noticed that we positioned `bee2` and `bee3` at the same height in the game world. We only need to push one of them horizontally to create a collision–perfect crash test dummies! We can use an **impulse** to create velocity for the outside bee.

Locate the `didMove` function in `GameScene.swift`. At the bottom, preceding all of our spawn code, add this line:

```
bee2.physicsBody?.applyImpulse(CGVector(dx: -3, dy: 0))
```

Run the project. You will see the outermost bee fly toward the middle and crash into the inner bee. This pushes the inner bee to the left and slows the first bee from the contact.

Attempt the same experiment with a variable: Increased mass. Before the impulse line, add this code to adjust the mass of `bee2`:

```
bee2.physicsBody?.mass = 0.2
```

Run the project. Hmm–our heavier bee does not move very far with the same impulse (it is a 200-gram bee, after all). It eventually bumps into the inner bee, but it is not a very exciting collision. We will need to crank up the impulse to propel our beefier bee. Change the impulse line to use a `dx` value of −25:

```
bee2.physicsBody?.applyImpulse(CGVector(dx: −25, dy: 0))
```

Run the project again. This time, our impulse provides enough energy to move the heavy bee in an interesting way. Notice how much energy the heavy bee transfers to the normal bee when they collide. Both bees possess enough momentum to eventually slide completely off the screen. Your simulator should look something like this screenshot, just before the bees slide off the screen:

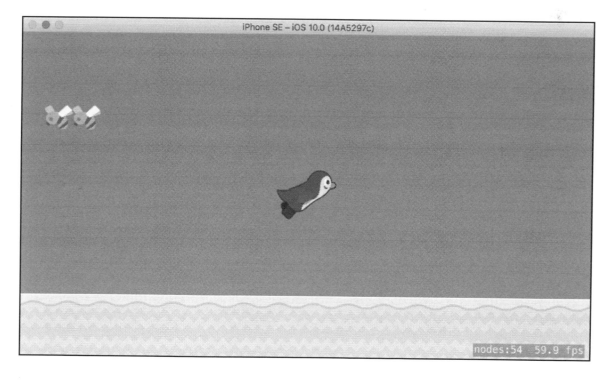

Before you move on, you may wish to experiment with the various physics properties that I outlined earlier in the chapter. You can create many collision variations; the physics simulation offers a lot of depth without much effort.

Impulse or force?

You have several options for moving nodes with physics bodies:

- An impulse is an immediate, one-time change to a physics body's velocity. In our test, an impulse gave the bee its velocity and it slowly bled speed to damping and its collision. Impulses are perfect for projectiles, such as missiles, bullets, disgruntled birds, and so on.
- A force applies velocity for only one physics calculation cycle. When we use a force, we typically apply it before every frame. Forces are useful for rocket ships, cars, or anything else that is continually self-propelled.
- You can also edit the `velocity` and `angularVelocity` properties of a body directly. This is useful for setting a manual velocity limit.

Checkpoint 3-B

We have made a number of structural changes to our project in this chapter. Feel free to download my project up to this point from `http://www.joyfulgames.io/chapter-3`

Summary

We have made great strides in this chapter. Our new class organization will serve us well over the course of this book. We learned how to use protocols to enforce commonality across classes, encapsulated our game objects into distinct classes, and explored tiling textures over the width of the ground node. Finally, we cleaned out some of our previous learning code from `GameScene` and used the new class system to spawn all of our game objects.

We also applied the physics simulation to our game. We have only scratched the surface of the powerful physics system in SpriteKit–we will dive deeper into custom collision events in Chapter 7, *Implementing Collision Events*–but we have already gained quite a bit of functionality. We explored the three types of physics bodies and studied the various physics properties you can use to fine-tune the physical behavior of your game objects. Then, we put all of our hard work into practice by bumping our bees together and watching the results.

Next, we will try several control schemes and move our player around the game world. This is an exciting addition; our project will begin to feel like a true game in Chapter 4, *Adding Controls*.

4
Adding Controls

Players control mobile games through a very limited number of interactions. Often, games feature only a single mechanic: tap anywhere on the screen to jump or fly. Contrast that with a console controller with dozens of button combinations. With so few actions, keeping users engaged with polished, fun controls is vital to the success of your game.

In this chapter, you will learn how to implement several popular control schemes that have emerged from the App Store. First, we will experiment with tilt controls; the physical orientation of the device will determine where the player flies. Then, we will wire up the `onTap` events on our sprite nodes. Finally, we will implement and polish a simple control scheme for flying in our game: tap anywhere on the screen to fly higher. You can combine these techniques to create unique and enjoyable controls in your future games.

The topics in this chapter include the following:

- Retrofitting the Player class for flight
- Polling for device movement with Core Motion
- Wiring up the sprite on Tap events
- Teaching our penguin to fly
- Improving the camera
- Looping the ground as the player moves forward

Retrofitting the Player class for flight

We need to perform a few quick setup tasks before we can react to player input. We will remove some of our older testing code and add a physics body to the `Player` class.

The Beekeeper

First, clean up the old bee physics tests from the last chapter. Open GameScene.swift, find didMove and locate the bottom two lines; one sets a mass for bee2, and the other applies an impulse to bee2. Remove these two lines:

```
bee2.physicsBody?.mass = 0.2
bee2.physicsBody?.applyImpulse(CGVector(dx: -25, dy: 0))
```

Updating the Player class

We need to give the Player class its own update function. We want to store player-related logic in Player and we need it to run before every frame:

1. Open Player.swift and add the following function inside Player:

   ```
   func update() { }
   ```

2. In GameScene.swift, add this code at the bottom of the GameScene class:

   ```
   override func update(_ currentTime: TimeInterval) {
       player.update()
   }
   ```

3. Perfect. The GameScene class will call the Player class's update function on every update.

Moving the ground

We initially placed the ground higher than necessary to make sure it displayed for all screen sizes in the previous chapter. We can now move the ground into its lower, final position since the player will soon move up and down, bringing the ground into view.

In GameScene.swift, locate the line that sets the ground.position value and change the y value from 150 to 30:

```
ground.position = CGPoint(x: -self.size.width * 2, y: 30)
```

Assigning a physics body to the player

We will use physics forces to move our player around the screen. To apply these forces, we must first add a physics body to the player sprite.

Creating a physics body shape from a texture

When gameplay allows, you should use circles to define your physics bodies–circles are the most efficient shape for the physics simulation and result in the highest frame rate. However, the accuracy of Pierre's shape is very important to our game play, and a circle is not a great fit for his shape. Instead, we will assign a special type of physics body, based on his texture.

Apple introduced the ability to define the shape of a physics body with opaque texture pixels in *Xcode 6*. This is a convenient addition as it allows us to create extremely accurate shapes for our sprites. There is a performance penalty, however it is computationally expensive to use these texture-driven physics bodies. You will want to use them sparingly, only on your most important sprites.

To create Pierre's physics body, add this code to `Player.swift`, at the bottom of the `init` function:

```
// Create a physics body based on one frame of Pierre's animation.
// We will use the third frame, when his wings are tucked in
let bodyTexture = textureAtlas.textureNamed("pierre-flying-3")
self.physicsBody = SKPhysicsBody(
    texture: bodyTexture, size: self.size)
// Pierre will lose momentum quickly with a high linearDamping:
self.physicsBody?.linearDamping = 0.9
// Adult penguins weigh around 30kg:
self.physicsBody?.mass = 30
// Prevent Pierre from rotating:
self.physicsBody?.allowsRotation = false
```

Run the project and the ground will appear to rise up to Pierre. Since we have given him a physics body, he is now subject to gravity. Pierre is actually dropping down the grid and the camera is adjusting to keep him centered. This is fine for now; we will give him the tools to fly into the sky later. Next, let's learn how to move a character, based on the tilt of the physical device.

Polling for device movement with Core Motion

Apple provides the **Core Motion** framework to expose precise information on the iOS device's orientation in physical space. We can use this data to move our player on the screen when the user tilts their device in the direction they want to move. This unique style of input offers new gameplay mechanics in mobile games.

 You will need a physical iOS device for this Core Motion section. The iOS simulator in Xcode does not simulate device movement. However, this section is only a learning exercise and is not required to finish the game we are building. Our final game will not use Core Motion. Feel free to skip the Core Motion section if you cannot test with a physical device.

Implementing the Core Motion code

It is very easy to poll for device orientation. We will check the device's position during every update and apply the appropriate force to our player. Follow these steps to implement the Core Motion controls:

1. In `GameScene.swift`, near the very top, add a new `import` statement after the `import SpriteKit` line:

   ```
   import CoreMotion
   ```

2. Inside the `GameScene` class, add a new constant named `motionManager` and instantiate an instance of `CMMotionManager`:

   ```
   let motionManager = CMMotionManager()
   ```

3. Inside the `GameScene` class `didMove` function, add the following code at the bottom. This lets Core Motion know that we want to poll the orientation data, so it needs to start reporting data:

   ```
   self.motionManager.startAccelerometerUpdates()
   ```

4. Finally, add the following code to the bottom of the `update` function to poll the orientation, build an appropriate vector, and apply a physical force to the player's character:

```
// Unwrap the accelerometer data optional:
if let accelData = self.motionManager.accelerometerData {
    var forceAmount:CGFloat
    var movement = CGVector()

    // Based on the device orientation, the tilt number
    // can indicate opposite user desires. The
    // UIApplication class exposes an enum that allows
    // us to pull the current orientation.
    // We will use this opportunity to explore Swift's
    // switch syntax and assign the correct force for the
    // current orientation:
    switch
        UIApplication.shared.statusBarOrientation {
    case .landscapeLeft:
        // The 20,000 number is an amount that felt right
        // for our example, given Pierre's 30kg mass:
        forceAmount = 20000
    case .landscapeRight:
        forceAmount = -20000
    default:
        forceAmount = 0
    }

    // If the device is tilted more than 15% towards
    // vertical, then we want to move the Penguin:
    if accelData.acceleration.y > 0.15 {
        movement.dx = forceAmount
    }
    // Core Motion values are relative to portrait view.
    // Since we are in landscape, use y-values for x-axis.
    else if accelData.acceleration.y < -0.15 {
        movement.dx = -forceAmount
    }

    // Apply the force we created to the player:
    player.physicsBody?.applyForce(movement)
}
```

Run the project. You can slide Pierre across the ice by tilting your device in the direction you want to move. Great work–we have successfully implemented our first control system.

Notice that Pierre falls through the ground when you move him too far in any direction. Later in the chapter, we will improve the ground, continuously repositioning it to cover the area beneath the player.

This is a simple example of using Core Motion data for player movement; we are not going to use this method in our final game. Still, you can extrapolate this example into advanced control schemes in your own games.

Checkpoint 4-A

To download my project, including the Core Motion code, visit this address: `http://www.joyfulgames.io/chapter-4`

Wiring up the sprite onTap events

Your games will often require the ability to run code when the player taps a specific sprite. I like to implement a system that includes all the sprites in your game so you can add tap events to each sprite without building any additional structure. We have already implemented `onTap` methods in all of our classes that adopt the `GameSprite` protocol; we still need to wire up the scene to call these methods when the player taps the sprites.

Before we move on, we need to remove the Core Motion code, since we will not be using it in the finished game. Once you finish exploring the Core Motion example, please remove it from the game by following the previous section's bullet points in reverse.

Implementing touchesBegan in the GameScene

SpriteKit calls our scene's touchesBegan function every time the screen is touched. We will read the location of the touch and determine the sprite node in that position. We can check if the touched node adopts our GameSprite protocol. If it does, this means it must have an onTap function, which we can then invoke. Add the touchesBegan function before the GameScene class I like to place it just after the didSimulatePhysics function:

```
override func touchesBegan(_ touches: Set<UITouch>,
    with event: UIEvent?) {
    for touch in (touches) {
        // Find the location of the touch:
        let location = touch.location(in: self)
        // Locate the node at this location:
        let nodeTouched = atPoint(location)
        // Attempt to downcast the node to the GameSprite protocol
        if let gameSprite = nodeTouched as? GameSprite {
            // If this node adheres to GameSprite, call onTap:
            gameSprite.onTap()
        }
    }
}
```

That is all we need to do to wire up all of the onTap functions we have implemented on the game object classes we have made. Of course, all of these onTap functions are empty at the moment; we will now add some functionality to illustrate the effect.

Larger than life

Open your Player.swift file and locate the onTap function. Temporarily, we will expand the penguin to a giant size when tapped, to demonstrate that we have wired our onTap functions correctly. Add this code inside the penguin's onTap function:

```
self.xScale = 4
self.yScale = 4
```

Run the project and tap on the penguin. Pierre will expand to four times his original size, as shown in the following screenshot:

This example shows that our `onTap` functions work. You can remove the scaling code you added to the `Player` class. We will keep the `onTap` wire-up code in `GameScene` so that we can use tap events later.

Teaching our penguin to fly

Let's implement the control scheme for our penguin. The player can tap anywhere on the screen to make Pierre fly higher and release to let him fall. We are going to make quite a few changes–if you need help, refer to the checkpoint at the end of this chapter. Start by modifying the `Player` class; follow these steps to prepare our `Player` for flight:

1. In `Player.swift`, add some new properties directly to the `Player` class:

```
// Store whether we are flapping our wings or in free-fall:
var flapping = false
// Set a maximum upward force.
// 57,000 feels good to me, adjust to taste:
let maxFlappingForce:CGFloat = 57000
// Pierre should slow down when he flies too high:
let maxHeight:CGFloat = 1000
```

2. So far, Pierre has been flapping his wings by default. Instead, we want to display the soaring animation by default and only run the flap animation when the user presses the screen. In the `init` function, remove the line that runs `flyAnimation` and, instead, run `soarAnimation`:

```
self.run(soarAnimation, withKey: "soarAnimation")
```

3. When the player touches the screen, we apply the upward force in the `Player` class's `update` function. Remember that `GameScene` calls the `Player` update function once per frame. Add this code in `update`:

```
// If flapping, apply a new force to push Pierre higher.
if self.flapping {
    var forceToApply = maxFlappingForce

    // Apply less force if Pierre is above position 600
    if position.y > 600 {
        // The higher Pierre goes, the more force we
        // remove. These next three lines determine the
        // force to subtract:
        let percentageOfMaxHeight = position.y / maxHeight
        let flappingForceSubtraction =
            percentageOfMaxHeight * maxFlappingForce
        forceToApply -= flappingForceSubtraction
    }
    // Apply the final force:
    self.physicsBody?.applyForce(CGVector(dx: 0, dy:
        forceToApply))
}

// Limit Pierre's top speed as he climbs the y-axis.
// This prevents him from gaining enough momentum to shoot
// over our max height. We bend the physics for game play:
if self.physicsBody!.velocity.dy > 300 {
    self.physicsBody!.velocity.dy = 300
}
```

4. Finally, we will provide two functions on `Player` to allow other classes to start and stop the flapping behavior. The `GameScene` class will call these functions when it detects touch input. Add the following functions to the `Player` class:

```
// Begin the flap animation, set flapping to true:
func startFlapping() {
    self.removeAction(forKey: "soarAnimation")
    self.run(flyAnimation, withKey: "flapAnimation")
    self.flapping - true
```

```
    }

    // Stop the flap animation, set flapping to false:
    func stopFlapping() {
        self.removeAction(forKey: "flapAnimation")
        self.run(soarAnimation, withKey: "soarAnimation")
        self.flapping = false
    }
```

Perfect, our `Player` is ready for flight. Now we will simply invoke the start and stop functions from the `GameScene` class.

Listening for touches in GameScene

The `SKScene` class (that `GameScene` inherits from) includes handy functions we can use to monitor touch input. Follow these steps to wire up the `GameScene` class:

1. In `GameScene.swift`, in the `touchesBegan` function, add this code at the very bottom to start the `Player` flapping when the user touches the screen:

   ```
   player.startFlapping()
   ```

2. After `touchesBegan`, create two new functions in the `GameScene` class. These functions stop the flapping when the user lifts his or her finger from the screen, or when an iOS notification interrupts the touch:

   ```
   override func touchesEnded(_ touches: Set<UITouch>,
       with event: UIEvent?) {
       player.stopFlapping()
   }

   override func touchesCancelled(_ touches: Set<UITouch>,
       with event: UIEvent?) {
       player.stopFlapping()
   }
   ```

Fine-tuning gravity

Before we test out our new flying code, we need to make one adjustment. The default gravity setting of 9.8 feels too real. Pierre lives in a cartoon world; real-world gravity is a bit of a drag. We can adjust gravity in the GameScene class; add this line at the bottom of the didMove function:

```
// Set gravity
self.physicsWorld.gravity = CGVector(dx: 0, dy: -5)
```

Spreading your wings

Run the project. Tap the screen to make Pierre fly higher; release to let him fall. Play with the action; Pierre rotates towards his vector and builds or loses momentum as you tap and release. Terrific! You have successfully implemented the core mechanic of our game. Take a minute to enjoy flying up and down, as in this screenshot:

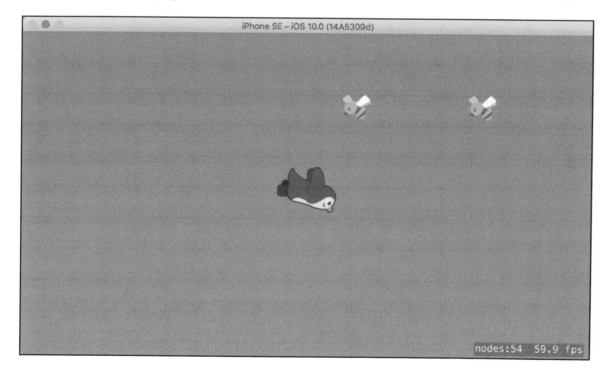

Improving the camera

Our camera code works well; it follows the player wherever they fly. However, we can improve the camera to enhance the flying experience. In this section, we will add two new features:

- Zoom the camera out as Pierre Penguin flies higher, reinforcing the feeling of increasing height.
- Suspend vertical centering when the player drops below the halfway point of the screen. This means the ground never fills too much of the screen, and adds the feeling of cutting upwards into the air when Pierre flies higher and the camera starts tracking him again.

Follow these steps to implement these two improvements:

1. In `GameScene.swift`, create a new variable in the `GameScene` class to store the center point of the screen:

```
var screenCenterY = CGFloat()
```

2. In the `didMove` function, set this new variable with the calculated center of the screen's height:

```
// Store the vertical center of the screen:
screenCenterY = self.size.height / 2
```

3. We need to rework the `didSimulatePhysics` function significantly. Remove the existing `didSimulatePhysics` function and replace it with this code:

```
override func didSimulatePhysics() {
    // Keep the camera locked at mid screen by default:
    var cameraYPos = screenCenterY
    cam.yScale = 1
    cam.xScale = 1

    // Follow the player up if higher than half the screen:
    if (player.position.y > screenCenterY) {
        cameraYPos = player.position.y
        // Scale out the camera as they go higher:
        let percentOfMaxHeight = (player.position.y -
            screenCenterY) / (player.maxHeight -
            screenCenterY)
        let newScale = 1 + percentOfMaxHeight
        cam.yScale = newScale
        cam.xScale = newScale
```

```
        }

        // Move the camera for our adjustment:
        self.camera!.position = CGPoint(x: player.position.x,
            y: cameraYPos)
    }
```

Run the project and then fly up. The world scales smaller as you gain height. The camera also now allows Pierre to dive below the center of the screen when you fly close to the ground. The following screenshot illustrates the two extremes. Notice the smaller sprites in the top screen; Pierre flies higher and the camera zooms out. In the bottom shot, the camera stops following Pierre vertically as he approaches the ground:

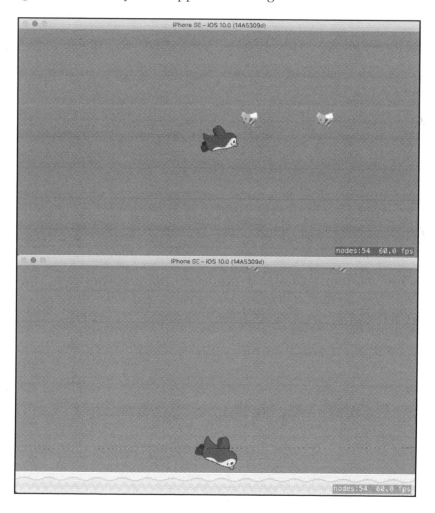

The combined effect adds a lot of polish to the game and increases the fun of flying. Our flying mechanic feels great. The next step is to move Pierre forward through the world.

Pushing Pierre forward

This style of game usually moves the world forward at a constant speed. Rather than applying force or impulse, we can manually set a constant velocity for Pierre during every update. Open the `Player.swift` file and add this code at the bottom of the `update` function:

```
// Set a constant velocity to the right:
self.physicsBody?.velocity.dx = 200
```

Run the project. Our protagonist penguin will move forward, past the swarm of bees and through the world. This works well, but you will quickly notice that the ground runs out as Pierre moves forward, as shown in this screenshot:

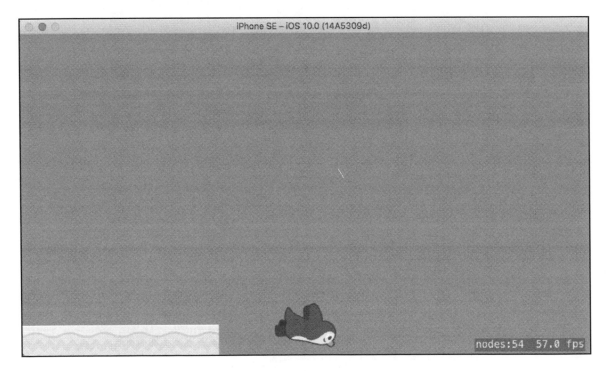

Recall that our ground is only as wide as the screen width multiplied by six. Rather than extending the ground further, we will move the ground's position at well-timed intervals. Since the ground is made from repeating tiles, there are many opportunities to jump its position forward seamlessly. We simply need to figure out when the player has travelled the correct distance.

Tracking the player's progress

First, we need to keep track of how far the player has flown. We will use this later as well, for keeping track of a high score. This is easy to implement. Follow these steps to track how far the player has flown:

1. In the `GameScene.swift` file, add two new properties to the `GameScene` class:

```
let initialPlayerPosition = CGPoint(x: 150, y: 250)
var playerProgress = CGFloat()
```

2. In the `didMove` function, update the line that positions the player to use the new `initialPlayerPosition` constant instead of the old hardcoded value:

```
// Add the player to the scene:
player.position = initialPlayerPosition
```

3. In the `didSimulatePhysics` function, update the new `playerProgress` property with the player's new distance:

```
// Keep track of how far the player has flown
playerProgress = player.position.x -
initialPlayerPosition.x
```

Perfect! We now have access to the player's progress at all times in the `GameScene` class. We can use the distance traveled to reposition the ground at the correct time.

Looping the ground

There are many possible methods to create an endless ground loop. We will implement a straightforward solution that jumps the ground forward after the player has travelled over roughly one third of its width. This method guarantees that the ground always covers the screen, given that our player starts in the middle third.

We will create the jump logic on the `Ground` class. Follow these steps to implement endless ground:

1. Open the `Ground.swift` file and add two new properties to the `Ground` class:

```
var jumpWidth = CGFloat()
// Note the instantiation value of 1 here:
var jumpCount = CGFloat(1)
```

2. In the `createChildren` function, we find the total width from one third of the children tiles and make it our `jumpWidth`. We will need to jump the ground forward every time the player travels this distance. You only need to add one line at the very bottom of the `createChildren` function:

```
// Save the width of one-third of the children nodes
jumpWidth = tileSize.width * floor(tileCount / 3)
```

3. Add a new function named `checkForReposition` to the `Ground` class, after the `createChildren` function. The scene will call this function before every frame to check whether we should jump the ground forward:

```
func checkForReposition(playerProgress:CGFloat) {
    // The ground needs to jump forward
    // every time the player has moved this distance:
    let groundJumpPosition = jumpWidth * jumpCount

    if playerProgress >= groundJumpPosition {
        // The player has moved past the jump position!
        // Move the ground forward:
        self.position.x += jumpWidth
        // Add one to the jump count:
        jumpCount += 1
    }
}
```

4. Open `GameScene.swift` and add this line at the bottom of the `didSimulatePhysics` function to call the `Ground` class's new logic:

```
// Check to see if the ground should jump forward:
ground.checkForReposition(playerProgress: playerProgress)
```

Run the project. The ground will seem to stretch on forever as Pierre flies forward. This looping ground is a big step towards the final game world. It may seem like a lot of work for a simple effect, but the looping ground is important, and our method will perform well on any screen size. Great work!

Checkpoint 4-B

To download my project up to this point, visit this address:
`http://www.joyfulgames.io/chapter-4`

Summary

In this chapter, we have transformed a tech demo into the beginnings of a real game. We have added a great deal of new code. You learned how to implement three distinct mobile game control methods: physical device motion, sprite tap events, and flying higher when the screen is touched. We polished the flying mechanic for maximum fun and sent Pierre flying forward through the world.

You also learned how to implement two common mobile game requirements: looping the ground and a smarter camera system. Both of these features make a big impact on our game.

Next, we will add more content to our level. Flying is already fun, but traveling past the first few bees feels a little lonely. We will give Pierre Penguin some company in `Chapter 5`, *Spawning Enemies, Coins, and Power-ups*.

5
Spawning Enemies, Coins, and Power-ups

One of the most enjoyable and creative aspects of game development is building the game world for your players to explore. Our young project is starting to resemble a playable game after adding the controls; the next step is to build more content. We will create additional classes for new enemies, collectible coins, and special Power-ups that give Pierre Penguin a boost as he navigates the perils of our world. We can then develop a system to spawn increasingly difficult patterns of these game objects as the player advances.

The topics in this chapter include the following:

- Adding the Power-up Star
- A new enemy – the Mad Fly
- Another terror – Bats!
- Guarding the ground with the Blade
- Adding coins
- Testing the new game objects

Introducing the cast

Strap on your hard hat as, we are going to be writing a lot of code in this chapter. Stick with it! The results are well worth the effort. Meet the new cast of characters we will be introducing in this chapter:

Locating and adding the art assets

Follow these steps to add these new art assets to the texture atlases in our `Assets.xcassets` file:

1. In Xcode, open the `Assets.xcassets` file and locate the texture atlases you have created. You should already have folders for `Enemies`, `Environment`, and `Pierre`.

2. Locate the `Enemies` folder in the downloadable asset bundle. You should see art for all of the enemies, including the Bat, the Blade, the Mad Fly, and the Bee.

3. We can skip the Bee art since we already added it to our project. Excluding the Bee, drag the rest of the asset files into the `Enemies` texture atlas in Xcode. You should be dragging 12 files into Xcode (two animation images per enemy, each with two resolutions). When you are done, your `Enemies` texture atlas should look like this:

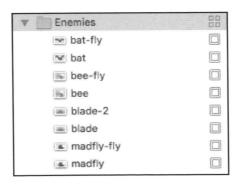

4. Great work! Now we just need to add the art for the two coins and the Power-up Star. Locate the `Environment` folder in the downloadable asset bundle and find the asset files for the Bronze Coin, the Gold Coin, and the Star. Just as before, drag the art for these three sprites into the `Environment` texture atlas in Xcode. You should be dragging six files into Xcode. You will end up with all of our Power-up art in the `Environment` folder. Your `Assets.xcassets` file should look like this when you are done:

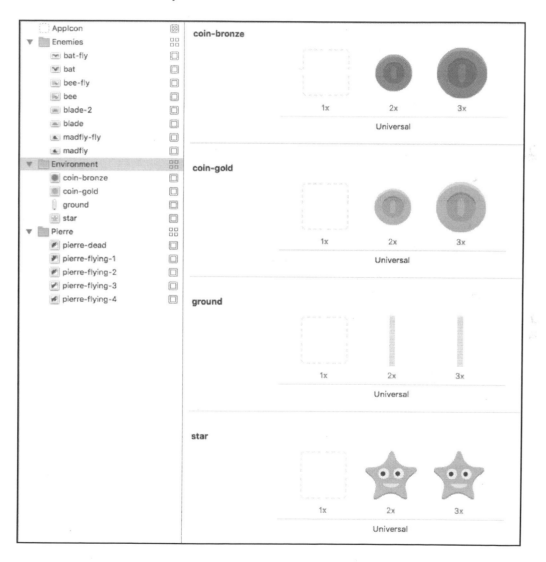

Terrific! We now have all of the art we need to create our enemies and Power-ups. Next, we will add the Star into the game.

Adding the Power-up Star

Many of my favorite games grant temporary invulnerability when the player picks up a Star. We will add a hyperactive Power-up Star to our game. Meet our Star:

Adding the Star class

Now that the art is in place, you can create a new Swift file named Star.swift in your project; we will continue to organize classes into distinct files. The Star class will be similar to the bee class we created earlier. It will inherit from SKSpriteNode and adhere to our GameSprite protocol. The Star will add a lot of power to the player, so we will also give it a special SKAction-based zany animation to make it stand out.

To create the Star class, add the following code in your Star.swift file:

```
import SpriteKit

class Star: SKSpriteNode, GameSprite {
    var initialSize = CGSize(width: 40, height: 38)
    var textureAtlas:SKTextureAtlas =
        SKTextureAtlas(named: "Environment")
    var pulseAnimation = SKAction()
```

```
init() {
    let starTexture =
        textureAtlas.textureNamed("star")
    super.init(texture: starTexture, color: .clear,
        size: initialSize)
    // Assign a physics body:
    self.physicsBody = SKPhysicsBody(circleOfRadius:
        size.width / 2)
    self.physicsBody?.affectedByGravity = false
    // Create our star animation and start it:
    createAnimations()
    self.run(pulseAnimation)
}

func createAnimations() {
    // Scale the star smaller and fade it slightly:
    let pulseOutGroup = SKAction.group([
        SKAction.fadeAlpha(to: 0.85, duration: 0.8),
        SKAction.scale(to: 0.6, duration: 0.8),
        SKAction.rotate(byAngle: -0.3, duration: 0.8)
        ])
    // Push the star big again, and fade it back in:
    let pulseInGroup = SKAction.group([
        SKAction.fadeAlpha(to: 1, duration: 1.5),
        SKAction.scale(to: 1, duration: 1.5),
        SKAction.rotate(byAngle: 3.5, duration: 1.5)
        ])
    // Combine the two into a sequence:
    let pulseSequence = SKAction.sequence([pulseOutGroup,
        pulseInGroup])
    pulseAnimation =
        SKAction.repeatForever(pulseSequence)
}

// Required to conform to protocols:
func onTap() {}
required init?(coder aDecoder: NSCoder) {
    super.init(coder: aDecoder)
}
}
```

Great! You should be familiar with most of this code at this point, since it is so similar to some of the other classes we have made. Let's continue by adding another new character: a grumpy fly.

Adding a new enemy – the Mad Fly

Pierre Penguin will need to dodge more than just Bees to accomplish his goal. We will add a few new enemies in this chapter, starting with the `MadFly` class. The Mad Fly is quite grumpy, as you can see:

Adding the MadFly class

`MadFly` is another straightforward class; it looks a lot like the `bee` code. Create a new Swift file named `MadFly.swift` and enter this code:

```
import SpriteKit

class MadFly: SKSpriteNode, GameSprite {
    var initialSize = CGSize(width: 61, height: 29)
    var textureAtlas:SKTextureAtlas =
        SKTextureAtlas(named: "Enemies")
    var flyAnimation = SKAction()

    init() {
        super.init(texture: nil, color: .clear,
            size: initialSize)
        self.physicsBody = SKPhysicsBody(circleOfRadius:
            size.width / 2)
        self.physicsBody?.affectedByGravity = false
        createAnimations()
        self.run(flyAnimation)
    }

    func createAnimations() {
        let flyFrames:[SKTexture] = [
            textureAtlas.textureNamed("madfly"),
            textureAtlas.textureNamed("madfly-fly")
        ]

        let flyAction = SKAction.animate(with: flyFrames,
            timePerFrame: 0.14)
```

```
        flyAnimation = SKAction.repeatForever(flyAction)
    }

    func onTap() {}
    required init?(coder aDecoder: NSCoder) {
        super.init(coder: aDecoder)
    }
}
```

Congratulations, you have successfully implemented the Mad Fly. No time to celebrate – onward to the Bats!

Another terror – Bats!

We are getting into quite a rhythm with creating new classes. Now, we will add a Bat to swarm with the Bees. The Bat is small, but has a very sharp fang:

Adding the Bat class

To add the Bat class, create a file named Bat.swift and add this code:

```
import SpriteKit

class Bat: SKSpriteNode, GameSprite {
    var initialSize = CGSize(width: 44, height: 24)
    var textureAtlas:SKTextureAtlas =
        SKTextureAtlas(named: "Enemies")
    var flyAnimation = SKAction()

    init() {
        super.init(texture: nil, color: .clear,
            size: initialSize)
        self.physicsBody = SKPhysicsBody(circleOfRadius:
            size.width / 2)
        self.physicsBody?.affectedByGravity = false
        createAnimations()
        self.run(flyAnimation)
```

```
    }

    func createAnimations() {
        let flyFrames:[SKTexture] = [
            textureAtlas.textureNamed("bat"),
            textureAtlas.textureNamed("bat-fly")
        ]
        let flyAction = SKAction.animate(with: flyFrames,
            timePerFrame: 0.12)
        flyAnimation = SKAction.repeatForever(flyAction)
    }

    func onTap() {}
    required init?(coder aDecoder: NSCoder) {
        super.init(coder: aDecoder)
    }
}
```

Now that you have created the Bat class, there is one more enemy to add. We will add the Blade class next.

Guarding the ground – adding the Blade

The Blade class will keep Pierre from flying too low. This enemy class will be similar to the others we have created, with one exception: we will generate a physics body based on the texture. The physics body circles that we have been using are much faster computationally and are usually sufficient to describe the shapes of our enemies; the Blade class requires a more complicated physics body, given its half-circle shape and bumpy edges:

Adding the Blade class

To add the `Blade` class, create a new file named `Blade.swift` and add the following code:

```swift
import SpriteKit

class Blade: SKSpriteNode, GameSprite {
    var initialSize = CGSize(width: 185, height: 92)
    var textureAtlas:SKTextureAtlas =
        SKTextureAtlas(named: "Enemies")
    var spinAnimation = SKAction()

    init() {
        super.init(texture: nil, color: .clear,
            size: initialSize)
        let startTexture = textureAtlas.textureNamed("blade")
        self.physicsBody = SKPhysicsBody(texture: startTexture,
            size: initialSize)
        self.physicsBody?.affectedByGravity = false
        self.physicsBody?.isDynamic = false
        createAnimations()
        self.run(spinAnimation)
    }

    func createAnimations() {
        let spinFrames:[SKTexture] = [
            textureAtlas.textureNamed("blade"),
            textureAtlas.textureNamed("blade-2")
        ]
        let spinAction = SKAction.animate(with: spinFrames,
            timePerFrame: 0.07)
        spinAnimation = SKAction.repeatForever(spinAction)
    }

    func onTap() {}
    required init?(coder aDecoder: NSCoder) {
        super.init(coder: aDecoder)
    }
}
```

Congratulations, the `Blade` class was the last enemy we needed to add to our game. This process may seem repetitive – you have written a lot of boilerplate code – but separating our enemies into their own classes allows each enemy to implement unique logic and behavior later. The benefits of this structure will become apparent as your games increase in complexity.

Next, we will add the class for our coins.

Adding the coins

Coins are more fun if there are two value variations. We will create two coins:

- A bronze coin, worth one coin
- A gold coin, worth five coins

The two coins will be distinguishable by their color, as seen here:

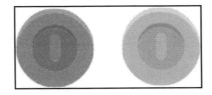

Creating the coin classes

We only need a single `Coin` class to create both denominations. Everything in the `Coin` class should look very familiar at this point. To create the `Coin` class, add a new file named `Coin.swift` and then enter the following code:

```swift
import SpriteKit

class Coin: SKSpriteNode, GameSprite {
    var initialSize = CGSize(width: 26, height: 26)
    var textureAtlas:SKTextureAtlas =
        SKTextureAtlas(named: "Environment")
    var value = 1

    init() {
        let bronzeTexture =
            textureAtlas.textureNamed("coin-bronze")
        super.init(texture: bronzeTexture, color: .clear,
            size: initialSize)
        self.physicsBody = SKPhysicsBody(circleOfRadius:
            size.width / 2)
        self.physicsBody?.affectedByGravity = false
    }

    // A function to transform this coin into gold!
    func turnToGold() {
        self.texture =
            textureAtlas.textureNamed("coin-gold")
```

```
        self.value = 5
    }

    func onTap() {}
    required init?(coder aDecoder: NSCoder) {
        super.init(coder: aDecoder)
    }
}
```

Great work – we have successfully added all of the new game objects we need for our final game!

Organizing the project navigator

You may notice that these new classes have cluttered the project navigator. This is a good time to clean up the navigator. Right-click the project in the project navigator and select **Sort by Type**, as shown in this screenshot:

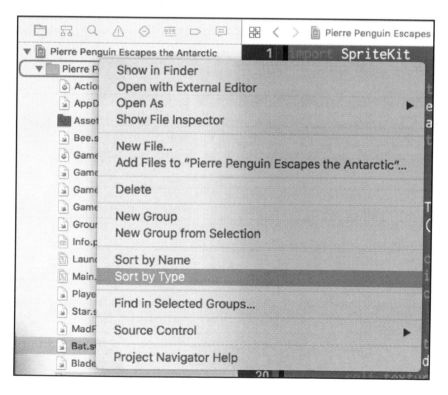

Your project navigator will segment itself by file type and sort into alphabetical order. This makes it much easier to find files as you need them.

Testing the new game objects

It is time to see our hard work in action. We will now add one instance of each of our new classes to the game. Note that we will remove this testing code after we are done; you may want to leave yourself a comment or extra space for easy removal. Open `GameScene.swift` and locate the six lines that spawn the existing bees. Add this code after the bee lines:

```swift
// Spawn a bat:
let bat = Bat()
bat.position = CGPoint(x: 400, y: 200)
self.addChild(bat)

// A blade:
let blade = Blade()
blade.position = CGPoint(x: 300, y: 76)
self.addChild(blade)

// A mad fly:
let madFly = MadFly()
madFly.position = CGPoint(x: 50, y: 50)
self.addChild(madFly)

// A bronze coin:
let bronzeCoin = Coin()
bronzeCoin.position = CGPoint(x: -50, y: 250)
self.addChild(bronzeCoin)

// A gold coin:
let goldCoin = Coin()
goldCoin.position = CGPoint(x: 25, y: 250)
goldCoin.turnToGold()
self.addChild(goldCoin)

// The powerup star:
let star = Star()
star.position = CGPoint(x: 250, y: 250)
self.addChild(star)
```

You may also wish to comment out the `Player` class line that moves Pierre forward, so the camera does not quickly move past your new game objects. Just make sure to uncomment it when you are done.

Once you are ready, run the project. You should see the entire family, as shown in the following screenshot:

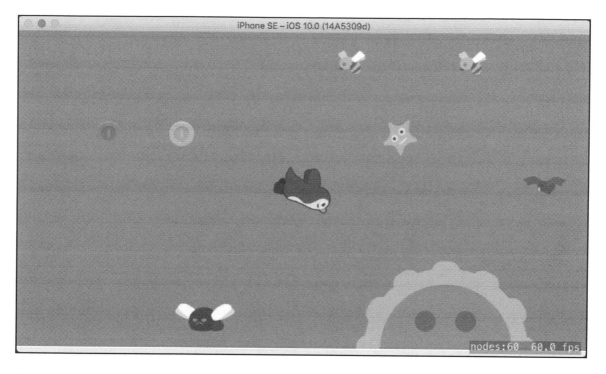

Terrific work! All of our code has paid off and we have a large cast of characters ready for action.

Checkpoint 5-A

To download my project to this point, browse to following URL:
http://www.joyfulgames.io/chapter-5

Preparing for endless flight

In Chapter 6, *Generating a Never-Ending World*, we will build a never-ending level by spawning tactical obstacle courses full of these new game objects. We need to clear out all of our test objects to get ready for this new level spawning system. Once you are ready, remove the new test code we just added to the GameScene class. Also, remove the six lines that we have been using to spawn the bees from previous chapters. Finally, uncomment the line in Player.swift that sets Pierre's velocity forward (if you chose to comment it out when testing the new classes in the previous section.)

When you are finished, your GameScene class didMove function should look like this:

```
override func didMove(to view: SKView) {
    self.anchorPoint = .zero
    self.backgroundColor = UIColor(red: 0.4, green: 0.6, blue:
        0.95, alpha: 1.0)

    // Assign the camera to the scene
    self.camera = cam

    // Add the ground to the scene:
    ground.position = CGPoint(x: -self.size.width * 2, y: 30)
    ground.size = CGSize(width: self.size.width * 6, height: 0)
    ground.createChildren()
    self.addChild(ground)

    // Add the player to the scene:
    player.position = initialPlayerPosition
    self.addChild(player)

    // Set gravity
    self.physicsWorld.gravity = CGVector(dx: 0, dy: -5)

    // Store the vertical center of the screen:
    screenCenterY = self.size.height / 2
}
```

When you run the project, you should only see Pierre and the ground, as shown here:

We are now ready to build our level.

Summary

You added the complete cast of characters to our game in this chapter. Look back at all that you accomplished; you added the Power-up Star, the bronze and gold coins, the Mad Fly, Bats, and the Blade. You tested all of the new classes and then removed the test code so that the project is ready for the level generation system we will put in place in the next chapter.

We put a lot of effort into building each new class. The world will come alive and reward our hard work in Chapter 6, *Generating a Never-Ending World*.

6

Generating a Never-Ending World

The unique challenge of an endless flyer-style game is in procedurally generating a rich, entertaining game world that extends as far as your player can fly. We will first explore level design concepts and tooling in Xcode; Apple added a built-in level designer to Xcode 6, allowing developers to arrange nodes visually within a scene. Once we become familiar with the SpriteKit level design methodology, we will create a custom solution to generate our world. In this chapter, you will build an entertaining world for our penguin game and learn to design and implement levels in SpriteKit for any genre of game.

The topics in this chapter include the following:

- Designing levels with the SpriteKit scene editor
- Building encounters for Pierre Penguin
- Integrating scenes into the game
- Looping encounters for a never-ending world
- Adding the Power-up Star at random
- Turning bronze coins to gold

Designing levels with the SpriteKit scene editor

The **Scene** editor is a valuable addition to SpriteKit. Previously, developers would be forced to hardcode positional values or rely on third-party tools or custom solutions for level design. Now, we can layout our levels directly within Xcode by dragging and dropping sprites. We can create nodes, attach physics bodies and constraints, create physics fields, and edit properties directly from the interface.

Here is a simple example scene you might build by simply clicking and dragging:

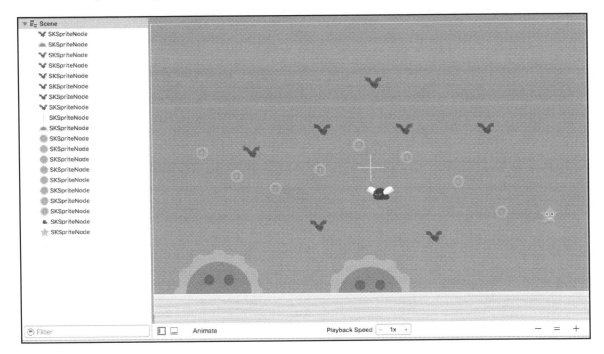

In this example, I simply dragged and positioned sprites in the scene. If you are making an unsophisticated game, you can start in the scene editor rather than creating custom classes. By editing physics bodies in the editor, you can even create entire physics-based games in the editor, adding only a few lines of code for the controls.

Complex games require custom logic and texture animation for every object, so we will implement a system in our penguin game that only uses the scene editor as a layout generation tool. We will write code to parse the layout data from the editor and turn it into fully functioning versions of the game classes we have created throughout this book. In this way, we will separate our game logic from our level data with minimal effort.

Separating level data from game logic

Level layout is data, and it is best to separate data from code. You increase flexibility by separating the level data into scene files. The benefits include the following:

- Non-technical contributors, such as artists and designers, can add and edit levels without changing any code.
- Iteration time improves since you do not need to run the game in the simulator each time you need to view your positional changes. Scene editor layouts provide immediate visual feedback.
- Each level is in a unique file, which is ideal for avoiding merge conflicts when using source control solutions such as Git.

Using custom classes in the scene editor

You can assign custom classes to the nodes you create in the scene editor. This assignment creates the association between scene editor node and custom class code (such as the `Bat`, `Blade`, `Coin`, and others that we created in Chapter 5, *Spawning Enemies, Coins, and Power-ups*).

You can also assign names to nodes in the scene editor and then query those names in your code. For example, we will create nodes with the custom class of `Coin` in the scene editor, and then assign the name of `GoldCoin` to the coins we want to turn gold. We will query for the name in the `Coin` class to fire the `turnToGold` function. We will see this technique in action later in the chapter.

Encounters in endless flying

Endless flyer games continue until the player loses. They do not feature distinct levels; instead, we will design **encounters** (my own term) for our protagonist penguin to explore. We can create an endless world by stringing together encounters one after the other and randomly recycling from the beginning when we need more content.

The following diagram illustrates the basic concept:

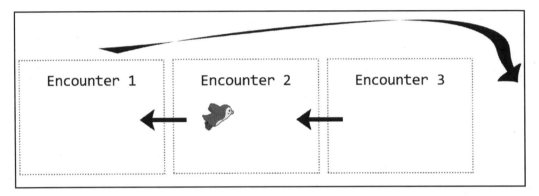

A finished game might include twenty or more encounters to feel varied and random. We will create three encounters in this chapter, to populate the encounter recycling system.

We will build each encounter in its own scene file, in the same way we would approach a separate level in a standard platformer or physics game.

Creating our first encounter

First, create an encounter folder group to keep our project organized. Right-click your project in the project navigator and create a new group named Encounters. Then, right-click on Encounters and add a new SpriteKitScene file (from the **iOS | Resource** category) named EncounterA.sks. Make sure to add a SpriteKitScene file and not a SceneKit scene (which is used in 3D games).

Xcode will add the new SpriteKitScene file to your project and open the scene editor. You should see a gray background with a white border, indicating the boundaries of the new scene. We can change the size of our scene to whatever we like; it will be easy to chain encounters together if each encounter is **900** pixels wide and **600** points tall.

You can easily change the scene's size values in the **Attributes inspector**. Towards the upper right corner of the scene editor, make sure you have the Attributes inspector open by selecting the middle icon, and then change the width and height, as shown in the following screenshot:

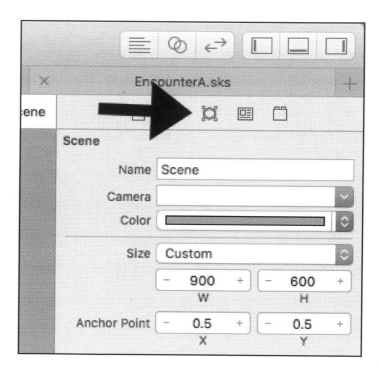

Next, we will create a `sprite` node, using the `Bat` custom class. Follow these steps to create a node in the scene editor:

1. You can drag textures from the media library directly onto the scene editor to create a new node. To open the media library, look towards the lower right side of the scene editor and select the movie reel icon, as shown in the following screenshot:

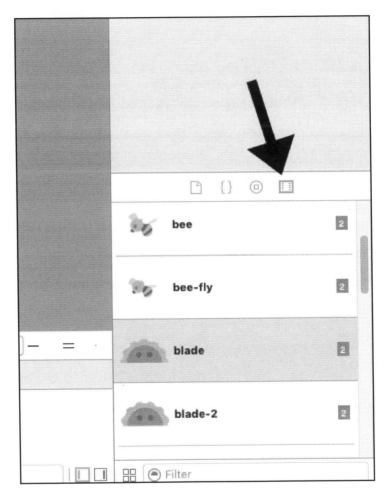

2. Scroll to the bat texture and drag it onto your scene. You will see a node appear on the gray background with the texture of the bat.

3. Using the **Custom Class** inspector on the upper right side, assign the `Bat` class to your node, as shown in this screenshot:

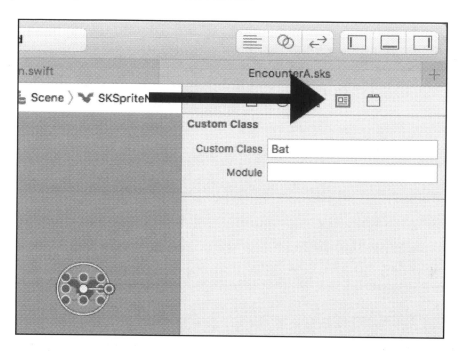

Great - you have started down the path to using the scene editor to create your level layout. We will repeat this process until we have built an entire encounter for Pierre Penguin to navigate. We can create Blades, Bees, Bats, Mad Flies, and Coins using this method.

Feel free to build out your first encounter. Add more nodes and assign custom classes until you are satisfied with the design. Try to picture the penguin character flying through the encounter. You do not need to add the ground or the Power-up Star; we will build both of those objects in our `GameScene` code.

You can speed up the build out by holding down the option key, then clicking and dragging from an existing node to create a copy. The copy will still have the same custom class attribute as the original. You can use this method to build the node layout very quickly.

It does not actually matter which texture you choose to drag onto the scene. The custom class attribute will determine which game object shows up in the final encounter. For instance, if you drag a bat texture onto the scene and assign it the custom class of Coin, you will see a coin in your game. However, dragging the correct texture helps you keep track of your progress and makes designing the layout easier.

In my encounter, I created a path through the bats, filled with gold coins. You can use my encounter, shown in the following screenshot, for inspiration:

Integrating scenes into the game

Next, we will create a new class to manage the encounters in our game. Add a new Swift file to your project and name it `EncounterManager.swift`. The `EncounterManager` class will loop through our encounter scenes and use the positional data to create the appropriate game object classes in the game world. Add the following code inside the new file:

```
import SpriteKit

class EncounterManager {
    // Store your encounter file names:
    let encounterNames:[String] = [
        "EncounterA"
    ]
    // Each encounter is an SKNode, store an array:
    var encounters:[SKNode] = []

    init() {
        // Loop through each encounter scene:
        for encounterFileName in encounterNames {
            // Create a new node for the encounter:
            let encounterNode = SKNode()

            // Load this scene file into a SKScene instance:
            if let encounterScene = SKScene(fileNamed:
                encounterFileName) {
                // Loop through each child node in the SKScene
                for child in encounterScene.children {
                    // Create a copy of the scene's child node
                    // to add to our encounter node:
                    let copyOfNode = type(of: child).init()
                    // Save the scene node's position to the copy:
                    copyOfNode.position = child.position
                    // Save the scene node's name to the copy:
                    copyOfNode.name = child.name
                    // Add the copy to our encounter node:
                    encounterNode.addChild(copyOfNode)
                }
            }

            // Add the populated encounter node to the array:
            encounters.append(encounterNode)
        }
    }

    // We will call this addEncountersToScene function from
    // the GameScene to append all of the encounter nodes to the
```

```
// world node from our GameScene:
func addEncountersToScene(gameScene:SKNode) {
    var encounterPosY = 1000
    for encounterNode in encounters {
        // Spawn the encounters behind the action, with
        // increasing height so they do not collide:
        encounterNode.position = CGPoint(x: -2000,
            y: encounterPosY)
        gameScene.addChild(encounterNode)
        // Double the Y pos for the next encounter:
        encounterPosY *= 2
    }
}
}
```

Great - you just added the functionality to use our scene file data inside the game world. Next, follow these steps to wire up the EncounterManager class in the GameScene class:

1. Add a new instance of the EncounterManager class as a constant in the GameScene class:

   ```
   let encounterManager = EncounterManager()
   ```

2. At the bottom of the didMove function, call addEncountersToScene to add each encounter node as a child of the GameScene node:

   ```
   encounterManager.addEncountersToScene(gameScene: self)
   ```

3. Since the EncounterManager class spawns encounters far off the screen, we will temporarily move our first encounter directly in front of the starting player position to test our code. Add this line in the didMove function:

   ```
   encounterManager.encounters[0].position =
       CGPoint(x: 400, y: 330)
   ```

Run the project. You will see Pierre flying through your new bat encounter. Your game should look something like this screenshot:

Congratulations, you have implemented the core functionality of using placeholder nodes in the scene editor. You can remove the line that positions this encounter at the beginning of the game, which we added in step 3. Next, we will create a system that repositions each encounter ahead of Pierre Penguin.

Checkpoint 6-A

You can download my project to this point at the following URL:
`http://www.joyfulgames.io/chapter-6`

Spawning endless encounters

We need at least three encounters to endlessly cycle and create a never-ending world; two can be on the screen at any one time and a third positioned ahead of the player. We can track Pierre's progress and reposition the encounter nodes ahead of him.

Building more encounters

We need to build at least two more encounters before we can implement the repositioning system. You can create more if you like; the system will support any number of encounters. For now, add two more SpriteKit Scene files to your game: `EncounterB.sks` and `EncounterC.sks`. Resize these scenes to 900 wide by 600 tall, like `EncounterA`. You can fill these encounters with bees, blades, coins, and bats – have fun! Make sure to assign the custom class attribute to the sprites that you drag into the scene editor.

For inspiration, here is my `EncounterB.sks`:

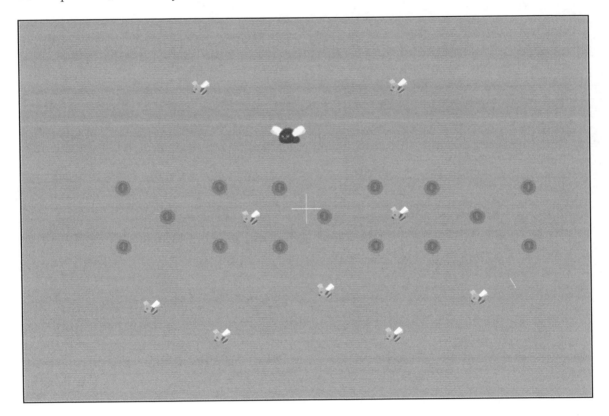

Here is my `EncounterC.sks`:

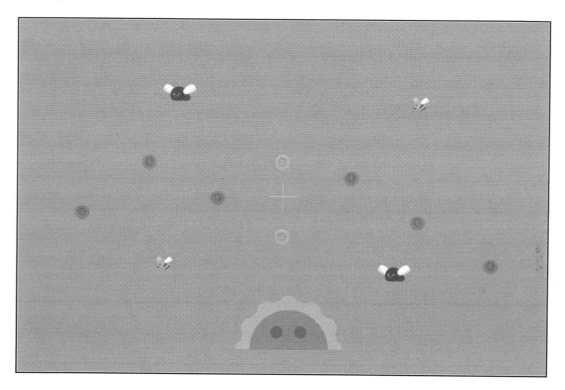

 For perfect alignment with the ground, place your `Blade` sprites at -224 on
the Y-axis.

Updating the EncounterManager class

We have to inform the `EncounterManager` class about these new encounters. Open the
`EncounterManager.swift` file and add the new encounter names to the `encounterNames`
constant:

```
// Store your encounter file names:
let encounterNames:[String] = [
    "EncounterA",
    "EncounterB",
    "EncounterC"
]
```

We also need to keep track of the encounters that can potentially be on the screen at any given time. Add two new properties to the `EncounterManager` class:

```
var currentEncounterIndex:Int?
var previousEncounterIndex:Int?
```

Storing metadata in SKSpriteNodeuserData property

We are going to recycle the encounter nodes as Pierre moves through the world, so we need to add the functionality to reset all of the game objects in an encounter before placing it in front of the player. Otherwise, Pierre's previous trips through the encounter would knock nodes out of place.

The `SKSpriteNode` class provides a property named `userData` that we can use to store any miscellaneous data about the sprite. We will use the `userData` property to store the initial position of each sprite in the encounter so we can reset the sprites when we reposition an encounter. Add these two new functions to the `EncounterManager` class:

```
// Store the initial positions of the children of a node:
func saveSpritePositions(node:SKNode) {
    for sprite in node.children {
        if let spriteNode = sprite as? SKSpriteNode {
            let initialPositionValue = NSValue.init(cgPoint:
                sprite.position)
            spriteNode.userData = ["initialPosition":
                initialPositionValue]
            // Save the positions for children of this node:
            saveSpritePositions(node: spriteNode)
        }
    }
}

// Reset all children nodes to their original position:
func resetSpritePositions(node:SKNode) {
    for sprite in node.children {
        if let spriteNode = sprite as? SKSpriteNode {
            // Remove any linear or angular velocity:
            spriteNode.physicsBody?.velocity = CGVector(dx: 0,
                dy: 0)
            spriteNode.physicsBody?.angularVelocity = 0
            // Reset the rotation of the sprite:
            spriteNode.zRotation = 0
            if let initialPositionVal =
```

```
            spriteNode.userData?.value(forKey:
                "initialPosition") as? NSValue {
            // Reset the position of the sprite:
            spriteNode.position =
                initialPositionVal.cgPointValue
        }

        // Reset positions on this node's children
        resetSpritePositions(node: spriteNode)
    }
  }
}
```

We want to call our new `saveSpritePositions` function on `init`, when we are first spawning the encounters. Update the `init` function of `EncounterManager` at the bottom of the `for` loop, below the line that appends the encounter node to the encounters array (the new line in bold):

```
// Add the populated encounter node to the array:
encounters.append(encounterNode)
// Save initial sprite positions for this encounter:
saveSpritePositions(node: encounterNode)
```

Lastly, we need a function to reset encounters and reposition them in front of the player. Add this new function to the `EncounterManager` class:

```
func placeNextEncounter(currentXPos:CGFloat) {
    // Count the encounters in a random ready type (Uint32):
    let encounterCount = UInt32(encounters.count)
    // The game requires at least 3 encounters to function
    // so exit this function if there are less than 3
    if encounterCount < 3 { return }

    // We need to pick an encounter that is not
    // currently displayed on the screen.
    var nextEncounterIndex:Int?
    var trulyNew:Bool?
    // The current encounter and the directly previous encounter
    // can potentially be on the screen at this time.
    // Pick until we get a new encounter
    while trulyNew == false || trulyNew == nil {
        // Pick a random encounter to set next:
        nextEncounterIndex =
            Int(arc4random_uniform(encounterCount))
        // First, assert that this is a new encounter:
        trulyNew = true
        // Test if it is instead the current encounter:
```

```
        if let currentIndex = currentEncounterIndex {
            if (nextEncounterIndex == currentIndex) {
                trulyNew = false
            }
        }
        // Test if it is the directly previous encounter:
        if let previousIndex = previousEncounterIndex {
            if (nextEncounterIndex == previousIndex) {
                trulyNew = false
            }
        }
    }

    // Keep track of the current encounter:
    previousEncounterIndex = currentEncounterIndex
    currentEncounterIndex = nextEncounterIndex

    // Reset the new encounter and position it ahead of the player
    let encounter = encounters[currentEncounterIndex!]
    encounter.position = CGPoint(x: currentXPos + 1000, y: 300)
    resetSpritePositions(node: encounter)
}
```

Wiring up EncounterManager in the GameScene class

We will track Pierre's progress in the `GameScene` class, and call the `EncounterManager` class code when appropriate. Follow these steps to wire up the `EncounterManager` class:

1. Add a new property to the `GameScene` class to track when we should next position an encounter in front of the player. We will start with a value of 150 to spawn the first encounter right away:

   ```
   var nextEncounterSpawnPosition = CGFloat(150)
   ```

2. Next, we simply need to check if the player moves past this position in the `didSimulatePhysics` function. Add this code at the bottom of `didSimulatePhysics`:

```
// Check to see if we should set a new encounter:
if player.position.x > nextEncounterSpawnPosition {
    encounterManager.placeNextEncounter(
        currentXPos: nextEncounterSpawnPosition)
    nextEncounterSpawnPosition += 1200
}
```

Fantastic – we have added all the functionality we need for endlessly looping encounters in front of the player. Run the project. You should see your encounters looping in front of you forever. Enjoy flying through your hard work!

 If you do not see your encounters, make sure that you assigned the Custom Class attribute in the scene editor for each node.

Spawning the Power-up Star at random

We still need to add the Power-p Star into the world. We can randomly spawn a Star every ten encounters to add some extra excitement. Follow these steps to add the Star logic:

1. Add a new instance of the `Star` class as a constant on the `GameScene` class:

```
let powerUpStar = Star()
```

2. Anywhere inside the `GameScene` `didMove` function, add the Star as a child of the `GameScene` and position it:

```
// Place the star out of the way for now:
self.addChild(powerUpStar)
powerUpStar.position = CGPoint(x: -2000, y: -2000)
```

3. Inside the `GameScene` `didSimulatePhysics` function, update your new encounter code as follows (new code in bold):

```
// Check to see if we should set a new encounter:
if player.position.x > nextEncounterSpawnPosition {
    encounterManager.placeNextEncounter(
        currentXPos: nextEncounterSpawnPosition)
```

```
nextEncounterSpawnPosition += 1200
// Each encounter has a 10% chance to spawn a star:
let starRoll = Int(arc4random_uniform(10))
if starRoll == 0 {
    // Only move the star if it is off the screen.
    if abs(player.position.x - powerUpStar.position.x)
        > 1200 {
        // Y Position 50-450:
        let randomYPos = 50 +
            CGFloat(arc4random_uniform(400))
        powerUpStar.position = CGPoint(x:
            nextEncounterSpawnPosition, y: randomYPos)
        // Remove any previous velocity and spin:
        powerUpStar.physicsBody?.angularVelocity = 0
        powerUpStar.physicsBody?.velocity =
            CGVector(dx: 0, dy: 0)
    }
}
```

Run the game again and you should see a Star spawn occasionally inside your encounters, as shown in the following screenshot:

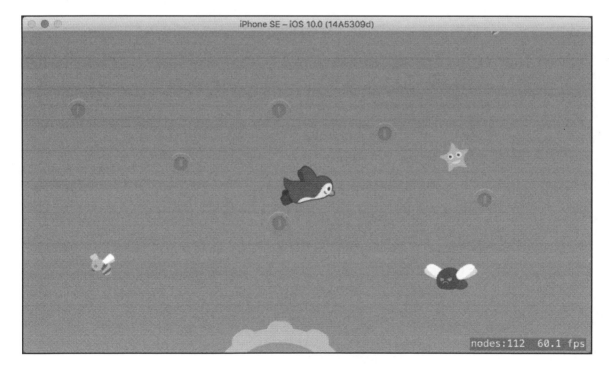

Turning bronze coins to gold

You may notice that your gold coins in the scene editor show up as bronze coins in the game. This is because the `Coin` class defaults to using the bronze texture and value. We will specify our gold coins by setting their name attribute to gold in the scene editor and then checking for this name in the `Coin init` function. Follow these steps to implement golden coins:

1. Open your encounters in the scene editor, select your gold coins, and use the Attributes inspector to set the name value of each node to `gold`, as shown here:

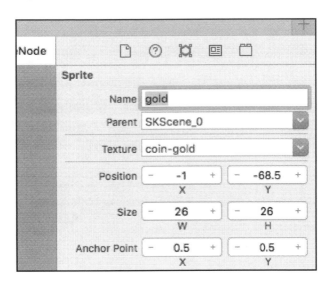

2. We can easily loop through all nodes with a certain name. We will use this functionality to run the `Coin` class's `turnToGold` function on any node with the name `gold`. Open `EncounterManager` and add the following code in the `init` function, at the bottom of the encounter `for` loop (new code in bold):

```
// Save initial sprite positions for this encounter:
saveSpritePositions(node: encounterNode)
// Turn golden coins gold!
encounterNode.enumerateChildNodes(withName: "gold") {
    (node: SKNode, stop: UnsafeMutablePointer) in
    (node as? Coin)?.turnToGold()
}
```

Run your project. The gold coins should be showing up correctly. Great work! This is a useful technique for passing extra data from the scene editor to the code.

Checkpoint 6-B

To download my project to this point, visit this URL:
http://www.joyfulgames.io/chapter-6

Summary

Great job – we have covered a lot of ground in this chapter. You learned about Xcode's new scene editor, used the scene editor to lay out sprites with custom classes, and interpreted the scene data to spawn game objects in our game world. Then, you created a system to loop encounters for our endless flyer game.

Congratulate yourself; the encounter system you built in this chapter is the most complex system in our game. You are officially in a great position to finish your first SpriteKit game!

Next, we will look at creating custom events when game objects collide. We will add health, damage, coin pick-up, invincibility, and more in Chapter 7, *Implementing Collision Events*.

7
Implementing Collision Events

So far, we have let the SpriteKit physics simulation detect and handle collisions between game objects. You have seen that Pierre Penguin sends enemies and coins flying off into space when he flies into them. This is because the physics simulation automatically monitors collisions and sets the post-collision trajectory and velocity of each colliding body. In this chapter, we will add our own game logic when two objects come into contact: taking damage from enemies, granting the player invulnerability after touching the star, and tracking points as the player collects coins. The game will become more fun to play as the game mechanics come to life.

The topics in this chapter include the following:

- Learning the SpriteKit collision vocabulary
- Adding contact events to our game
- Player health and damage
- Collecting coins
- The Power-up Star logic

Learning the SpriteKit collision vocabulary

SpriteKit uses some unique concepts and terms to describe physics events. If you familiarize yourself with these terms now, it will be easier to understand the implementation steps later in the chapter.

Collision versus contact

There are two types of interactions when physics bodies come together in the same space:

- **Collision**: This is the physics simulation's mathematical analysis and repositioning of bodies after they touch. Collisions include all the automatic physical interactions between bodies: preventing overlap, bouncing apart, spinning through the air, and transferring momentum. By default, physics bodies collide with every other physics body in the scene; we have witnessed this automatic collision behavior in our game so far.

- **Contact:** This event also occurs when two bodies touch. Contact events allow us to wire in our custom game logic when two bodies come into contact. Contact events do not create any change on their own; they only provide us with the chance to execute our own code. For instance, we will use contact events to assign damage to the player when he or she runs into an enemy. There are no contact events by default; we will manually configure contacts in this chapter.

Physics bodies collide with every other body in the scene by default, but you can configure specific bodies to ignore collisions and pass through each other without any physical reaction.

Additionally, collisions and contacts are independent; you can disable physical collision between two types of bodies and still fire custom code with a contact event when the bodies pass through each other.

Physics category masks

You can assign physics categories to each physics body in your game. These categories allow you to specify the bodies that should collide, the bodies that should contact, and the bodies that should pass through each other without any event. When two bodies try to share the same space, the physics simulation will compare each body's categories and test if collision or contact events should fire.

Our game will include physics categories for the penguin, the ground, the coins, and the enemies.

Physics categories are stored as 32-bit masks, which allow the physics simulation to perform these tests with processor-efficient bitwise operations. It is not strictly necessary to understand bitwise operations to use physics categories, but it is a nice topic for further reading, if you are interested in enhancing your knowledge. If you are interested, try an Internet search for *swift bitwise operations*.

Each physics body has three properties you can use to control collisions in your game. Let's begin with a very simple summary of each property, and then explore them in depth:

- `categoryBitMask`: The physics body's own physical categories
- `collisionBitMask`: Collide with these physical categories
- `contactTestBitMask`: Contact with these physical categories

The `categoryBitMask` property stores the body's current physics categories. The default value is `0xFFFFFFFF`, equating to every category. This means that, by default, every physics body belongs to every physics category.

The `collisionBitMask` property specifies the physical categories the body should collide with, preventing two bodies from sharing the same space. The starting value is `0xFFFFFFFF`, or all bits set, meaning that the body will collide with every category by default. When one body begins to overlap with another, the physics simulation compares each body's `collisionBitMask` against the other body's `categoryBitMask`. If there is a match, a collision takes place. Note that this test works two ways; each body can independently participate or ignore a collision.

The `contactTestBitMask` property works just like the collision property, but specifies categories for contact events, instead of collisions. The default value is `0x00000000`, or no bits set, meaning that the body will not contact with anything by default.

This is a dense subject. It is ok to move forward if you do not yet fully understand this topic. Implementing category masks into our game will help you learn.

Using category masks in Swift

Apple's Adventure game demo provides a good implementation of bitmasks in Swift. You can download Apple's latest demo SpriteKit games by visiting `https://developer.apple.com/spritekit/`. We will follow their example and use an `enum` to store our categories as `UInt32` values, writing these bitmasks in an easy-to-read manner. The following is an example of a physics category `enum` for a theoretical war game:

```
enum PhysicsCategory:UInt32 {
```

```
        case playerTank = 1
        case enemyTanks = 2
        case missiles = 4
        case bullets = 8
        case buildings = 16
}
```

It is very important to double the value for each subsequent group; this is a necessary step to create proper bitmasks for the physics simulation. For example, if we were to add fighterJets, the value would need to be 32. Always remember to double subsequent values to create unique bitmasks that perform as expected in the physics tests.

 Bitmasks are binary values that the CPU can very quickly compare to check for a match. You do not need to understand bitwise operators to complete this material, but if you are already familiar and curious, this doubling method works because 2 is equivalent to 1 << 1 (binary: 10), 4 is equivalent to 1 << 2 (binary: 100), 8 is equivalent to 1 << 3 (binary: 1000), and so on. We opt for the manual doubling since enum values must be literals, and these values are easier for humans to read.

Adding contact events to our game

Now that you are familiar with SpriteKit's physics concepts, we can head into Xcode to implement physics categories and contact logic for our penguin game. We will start by adding our physics categories.

Setting up the physics categories

To create our physics categories, open your GameScene.swift file and enter the following code at the very bottom, completely outside the GameScene class:

```
enum PhysicsCategory:UInt32 {
    case penguin = 1
    case damagedPenguin = 2
    case ground = 4
    case enemy = 8
    case coin = 16
    case powerup = 32
}
```

Notice how we double each succeeding value, as in our previous example. We are also creating an extra category for our penguin to use after he takes damage. We will use the `damagedPenguin` physics category to allow the penguin to pass through enemies for a few seconds after taking damage.

Assigning categories to game objects

Now that we have the physics categories, we need to go back through our existing game objects and assign the categories to the physics bodies. We will start with the `Player` class.

The player

Open `Player.swift` and add the following code at the bottom of the `init` function:

```
self.physicsBody?.categoryBitMask =
    PhysicsCategory.penguin.rawValue
self.physicsBody?.contactTestBitMask =
    PhysicsCategory.enemy.rawValue |
    PhysicsCategory.ground.rawValue |
    PhysicsCategory.powerup.rawValue |
    PhysicsCategory.coin.rawValue
self.physicsBody?.collisionBitMask =
    PhysicsCategory.ground.rawValue
```

We assigned the penguin physics category to the `Player` physics body, and used the `contactTestBitMask` property to set up contact logic tests with enemies, the ground, Power-ups, and coins. We used the `collisionBitMask` to make the penguin only bounce off the ground while gliding through other game objects.

Also, notice how we use the `rawValue` property of our `enum` values. You will need to use the `rawValue` property whenever you are using the physics category bitmasks.

The ground

Next, let's assign the physics category for the `Ground` class. Open `Ground.swift`, and add the following code at the very bottom of the `createChildren` function:

```
self.physicsBody?.categoryBitMask =
    PhysicsCategory.ground.rawValue
```

All we need to do is assign the ground bitmask to the `Ground` class physics body, since it already collides with everything by default.

The Power-up Star

Open `Star.swift` and add the following code at the bottom of the `init` function:

```
self.physicsBody?.categoryBitMask =
    PhysicsCategory.powerup.rawValue
```

This assigns the Power-up physics category to the `Star` class.

Enemies

Perform this same action in `Bat.swift`, `Bee.swift`, `Blade.swift`, and `MadFly.swift`. Add the following code inside their `init` functions:

```
self.physicsBody?.categoryBitMask = PhysicsCategory.enemy.rawValue
self.physicsBody?.collisionBitMask =
    ~PhysicsCategory.damagedPenguin.rawValue
```

We use the bitwise NOT operator (~) to remove the `damagedPenguin` physics category from collisions with enemies. Enemies will collide with all categories except the `damagedPenguin` physics category. This allows us to change the penguin's category to the `damagedPenguin` value when we want the penguin to ignore enemy collisions and pass straight through.

Coins

Lastly, we will add the coin physics category. We do not want coins to collide with other game objects, but we still want to monitor for contact events. Open `Coin.swift` and add the following code at the bottom of the `init` function:

```
self.physicsBody?.categoryBitMask = PhysicsCategory.coin.rawValue
self.physicsBody?.collisionBitMask = 0
```

Preparing GameScene for contact events

Now that we have assigned the physics categories to our game objects, we can monitor for contact events in the GameScene class. Follow these steps to wire up the GameScene class:

1. First, we need to tell the GameScene class to implement the SKPhysicsContactDelegate protocol. SpriteKit can then inform the GameScene class when contact events occur. Change the GameScene class declaration line to look like this:

   ```
   class GameScene: SKScene, SKPhysicsContactDelegate {
   ```

2. We will tell SpriteKit to inform GameScene of contact events by setting the GameScene physicsWorld contactDelegate property to the GameScene instance. At the bottom of the GameScene didMove function, add this line:

   ```
   self.physicsWorld.contactDelegate = self
   ```

3. SKPhysicsContactDelegate defines a didBegin function that will fire when contact occurs. We can now implement this didBegin function in the GameScene class. Create a new function in the GameScene class named didBegin, as shown in the following code:

   ```
   func didBegin(_ contact: SKPhysicsContact) {
       // Each contact has two bodies,
       // We do not know which is which.
       // We will find the penguin body first, then use
       // the other body to determine the type of contact.
       let otherBody:SKPhysicsBody
       // Combine the two penguin physics categories into one
       // bitmask using the bitwise OR operator |
       let penguinMask = PhysicsCategory.penguin.rawValue |
           PhysicsCategory.damagedPenguin.rawValue
       // Use the bitwise AND operator & to find the penguin.
       // This returns a positive number if body A's category
       // is the same as either the penguin or damagedPenguin:
       if (contact.bodyA.categoryBitMask & penguinMask) > 0 {
           // bodyA is the penguin, we will test bodyB's type:
           otherBody = contact.bodyB
       }
       else {
           // bodyB is the penguin, we will test bodyA's type:
           otherBody = contact.bodyA
       }
       // Find the type of contact:
   ```

```
switch otherBody.categoryBitMask {
case PhysicsCategory.ground.rawValue:
    print("hit the ground")
case PhysicsCategory.enemy.rawValue:
    print("take damage")
case PhysicsCategory.coin.rawValue:
    print("collect a coin")
case PhysicsCategory.powerup.rawValue:
    print("start the power-up")
default:
    print("Contact with no game logic")
}
}
```

This function will serve as a central hub for our contact events. We will print to the console when our various contact events occur, to test that our code is working.

Viewing console output

You can use the `print` function to write information to the console, which is very useful for debugging. If you have not yet used the console in Xcode, follow these simple steps to view it:

1. In the upper right-hand corner of Xcode, make sure the debug area is turned on, as shown in the following screenshot:

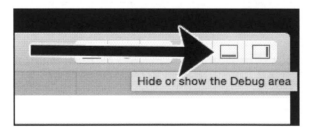

2. In the bottom right-hand corner of Xcode, make sure the console is turned on, as shown in the following screenshot:

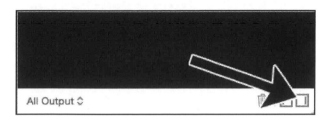

Testing our contact code

Now that you can see your console output, run the project. You should see our `print` strings appear in the console as you fly Pierre into various game objects. Your console should look something like this:

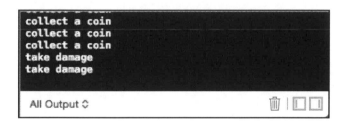

Congratulations – if you see the contact output in the console, you have completed the structure for our contact system.

You may notice that flying into coins produces strange collision behavior, which we will enhance later in the chapter. Next, we will add game logic for each type of contact.

Checkpoint 7-A

To download my project to this point, visit the following URL:
http://www.joyfulgames.io/chapter-7

Player health and damage

The first custom contact logic is player damage. We will assign the player health points and take them away when damaged. The game will end when the player runs out of health. This is one of the core mechanics of our gameplay. Follow these steps to implement the health logic:

1. In the `Player.swift` file, add six new properties to the `Player` class:

```
// The player will be able to take 3 hits before game over:
var health:Int = 3
// Keep track of when the player is invulnerable:
var invulnerable = false
// Keep track of when the player is newly damaged:
var damaged = false
// We will create animations to run when the player takes
// damage or dies. Add these properties to store them:
var damageAnimation = SKAction()
var dieAnimation = SKAction()
// We want to stop forward velocity if the player dies,
// so we will now store forward velocity as a property:
var forwardVelocity:CGFloat = 200
```

2. Inside the `update` function, change the code that moves the player through the world to use the new `forwardVelocity` property:

```
// Set a constant velocity to the right:
self.physicsBody?.velocity.dx = self.forwardVelocity
```

3. At the very beginning of the `startFlapping` function, add this line to prevent the player from flying higher when dead:

```
if self.health <= 0 { return }
```

4. Add the same line at the very beginning of the `stopFlapping` function to prevent the soar animation from running after death:

```
if self.health <= 0 { return }
```

5. Add a new function named `die` to the `Player` class:

```
func die() {
    // Make sure the player is fully visible:
    self.alpha = 1
    // Remove all animations:
    self.removeAllActions()
```

```
        // Run the die animation:
        self.run(self.dieAnimation)
        // Prevent any further upward movement:
        self.flapping = false
        // Stop forward movement:
        self.forwardVelocity = 0
    }
```

6. Add a new function named `takeDamage` to the `Player` class:

```
func takeDamage() {
    // If invulnerable or damaged, return:
    if self.invulnerable || self.damaged { return }

    // Remove one from our health pool
    self.health -= 1
    if self.health == 0 {
        // If we are out of health, run the die function:
        die()
    }
    else {
        // Run the take damage animation:
        self.run(self.damageAnimation)
    }
}
```

7. Open the `GameScene.swift` file. Inside the `didBegin` function, update the switch case that fires when contact is made with an enemy:

```
case PhysicsCategory.enemy.rawValue:
    print("take damage")
    player.takeDamage()
```

8. We will also take damage when we hit the ground. Update the ground case in the same way:

```
case PhysicsCategory.ground.rawValue:
    print("hit the ground")
    player.takeDamage()
```

Good work – let's test our code to make sure everything is working correctly. Run the project and smash into some enemies. You can watch the printed output in the console to make sure everything is working correctly. After taking damage three times, the penguin should drop to the ground and become unresponsive.

You may notice that there is no way for the player to tell how many health points he or she has remaining as they play the game. We will add a health meter to the scene in the next chapter.

Next, we will enhance the feel of the game with new animations when the player takes damage and when the game ends.

Animations for damage and game over

We will use SKAction sequences to create fun animations when the player takes damage. By combining actions, we will grant temporary safety in a damaged state after the player hits an enemy. We will show a fade animation that slowly pulses at first and then speeds up as the safe state starts to wear off.

The damage animation

To add the new animation, add this code at the bottom of the Player class createAnimations function:

```
// --- Create the taking damage animation ---
let damageStart = SKAction.run {
    // Allow the penguin to pass through enemies:
    self.physicsBody?.categoryBitMask =
        PhysicsCategory.damagedPenguin.rawValue
}
// Create an opacity pulse, slow at first and fast at the end:
let slowFade = SKAction.sequence([
    SKAction.fadeAlpha(to: 0.3, duration: 0.35),
    SKAction.fadeAlpha(to: 0.7, duration: 0.35)
    ])
let fastFade = SKAction.sequence([
    SKAction.fadeAlpha(to: 0.3, duration: 0.2),
    SKAction.fadeAlpha(to: 0.7, duration: 0.2)
    ])
let fadeOutAndIn = SKAction.sequence([
    SKAction.repeat(slowFade, count: 2),
    SKAction.repeat(fastFade, count: 5),
    SKAction.fadeAlpha(to: 1, duration: 0.15)
    ])
// Return the penguin to normal:
let damageEnd = SKAction.run {
    self.physicsBody?.categoryBitMask =
```

```
        PhysicsCategory.penguin.rawValue
    // Turn off the newly damaged flag:
    self.damaged = false
}
// Store the whole sequence in the damageAnimation property:
self.damageAnimation = SKAction.sequence([
    damageStart,
    fadeOutAndIn,
    damageEnd
    ])
```

Next, update the `takeDamage` function to flag the player as damaged, immediately after taking a hit. The damage animation you just created will turn the damaged flag back off once it has completed. After this change, the first four lines of the `takeDamage` function should look like this (the new code is written in bold):

```
// If invulnerable or damaged, return out of the function:
if self.invulnerable || self.damaged { return }
// Set the damaged state to true after being hit:
self.damaged = true
```

Run the project. Directly after taking damage, your penguin should fade and be able to pass through enemies, as shown in this image:

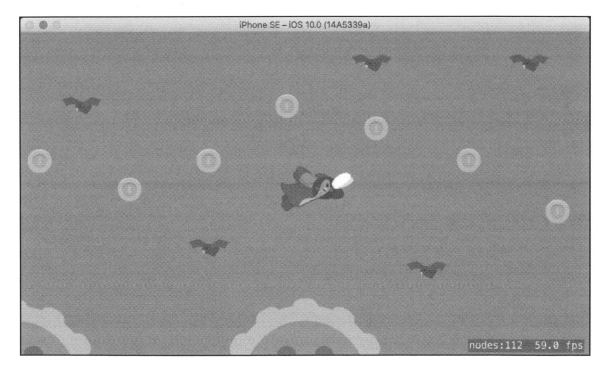

We are starting to see some good results from our hard work. Notice how the penguin can pass through enemies but still collides with coins, the star, and the ground while in the invulnerable state. Next, we will add a game over animation.

The game over animation

We will create a funny, over-the-top death animation when the penguin runs out of health. When Pierre loses his last hit point, he will hang in the air, scale larger, flip over on to his back, and then finally fall to the ground. To implement this animation, add the following code at the bottom of the `Player` class `createAnimations` function:

```
/* --- Create the death animation --- */
let startDie = SKAction.run {
    // Switch to the death texture with X eyes:
    self.texture =
        self.textureAtlas.textureNamed("pierre-dead")
    // Suspend the penguin in space:
    self.physicsBody?.affectedByGravity = false
    // Stop any movement:
    self.physicsBody?.velocity = CGVector(dx: 0, dy: 0)
}

let endDie = SKAction.run {
    // Turn gravity back on:
    self.physicsBody?.affectedByGravity = true
}

self.dieAnimation = SKAction.sequence([
    startDie,
    // Scale the penguin bigger:
    SKAction.scale(to: 1.3, duration: 0.5),
    // Use the waitForDuration action to provide a short pause:
    SKAction.wait(forDuration: 0.5),
    // Rotate the penguin on to his back:
    SKAction.rotate(toAngle: 3, duration: 1.5),
    SKAction.wait(forDuration: 0.5),
    endDie
    ])
```

Run the project and bump into three enemies. You will see the comedic death animation play, as shown in the following screenshot:

Poor Pierre Penguin! Good job implementing the damage and death animations. Next, we will handle coin collection on the coin contact event.

Collecting coins

As the main goal for the player, collecting coins should be one of the most enjoyable aspects of our game. We will create a rewarding animation when the player contacts a coin. Follow these steps to implement coin collection:

1. In GameScene.swift, add a new property to the GameScene class:

   ```
   var coinsCollected = 0
   ```

2. In Coin.swift, add a new function to the Coin class named collect:

   ```
   func collect() {
       // Prevent further contact:
       self.physicsBody?.categoryBitMask = 0
   ```

```
    // Fade out, move up, and scale up the coin:
    let collectAnimation = SKAction.group([
        SKAction.fadeAlpha(to: 0, duration: 0.2),
        SKAction.scale(to: 1.5, duration: 0.2),
        SKAction.move(by: CGVector(dx: 0, dy: 25),
            duration: 0.2)
        ])
    // After fading it out, move the coin out of the way
    // and reset it to initial values until the encounter
    // system re-uses it:
    let resetAfterCollected = SKAction.run {
        self.position.y = 5000
        self.alpha = 1
        self.xScale = 1
        self.yScale = 1
        self.physicsBody?.categoryBitMask =
            PhysicsCategory.coin.rawValue
    }
    // Combine the actions into a sequence:
    let collectSequence = SKAction.sequence([
        collectAnimation,
        resetAfterCollected
        ])
    // Run the collect animation:
    self.run(collectSequence)
}
```

3. In `GameScene.swift`, call the new `collect` function from the coin contact case in the `didBegin` function:

```
case PhysicsCategory.coin.rawValue:
    // Try to cast the otherBody's node as a Coin:
    if let coin = otherBody.node as? Coin {
        // Invoke the collect animation:
        coin.collect()
        // Add the value of the coin to our counter:
        self.coinsCollected += coin.value
        print(self.coinsCollected)
    }
```

Great work! Run the project and try to collect some coins. You will see the coins perform their collection animation. The game will keep track of how many coins you are collecting and print the number to the console. The player cannot see that number yet; we will add a text counter on the game screen in the next chapter. Next, we will implement the Power-up Star game logic.

The Power-up Star logicterrific progress in this chapter. To download my project up to this

When the player contacts the star, we will grant invulnerability for a short time and give the player great speed to power through encounters. Follow these steps to implement the Power-up:

1. In `Player.swift`, add a new function to the `Player` class, as shown here:

```swift
func starPower() {
    // Remove any existing star power-up animation, if
    // the player is already under the power of star
    self.removeAction(forKey: "starPower")  ·
    // Grant great forward speed:
    self.forwardVelocity = 400
    // Make the player invulnerable:
    self.invulnerable = true
    // Create a sequence to scale the player larger,
    // wait 8 seconds, then scale back down and turn off
    // invulnerability, returning the player to normal:
    let starSequence = SKAction.sequence([
        SKAction.scale(to: 1.5, duration: 0.3),
        SKAction.wait(forDuration: 8),
        SKAction.scale(to: 1, duration: 1),
        SKAction.run {
            self.forwardVelocity = 200
            self.invulnerable = false
        }
        ])
    // Execute the sequence:
    self.run(starSequence, withKey: "starPower")
}
```

2. Invoke the new function from the `GameScene` class `didBegin` function, under the Power-up case:

```swift
case PhysicsCategory.powerup.rawValue:
    player.starPower()
```

You may find it helpful to increase the spawn rate of the Power-up Star in order to test. Remember that we are generating a random number in the `didSimulatePhysics` function of `GameScene` to determine how often we spawn the star. To spawn the star more often, comment out the line that generates a random number and replace it with a hardcoded 0, as shown here (the new code is written in bold):

```
//let starRoll = Int(arc4random_uniform(10))
let starRoll = 0
if starRoll == 0 {
```

Great! Now it will be easy to test the Power-up Star. Run the project and find a star. The penguin should scale to a large size and start charging forward, blowing enemies aside as he passes, as shown here:

Remember to change the star-spawning code back to a random number before you continue, or the star will spawn too often.

Checkpoint 7-B

We have made terrific progress in this chapter. To download my project up to this point, visit this URL:

`http://www.joyfulgames.io/chapter-7`

Summary

Our penguin game is looking great! You have brought the core mechanics to life by implementing the sprite contact events. You learned how SpriteKit handles collisions and contacts, used bitmasks to assign collision categories to different types of sprites, wired up a contact system in our penguin game, and added custom game logic for taking damage, collecting coins, and gaining the Power-up Star.

We have a playable game at this point; the next step is adding polish, menus, and features to make the game stand out. We will make our game shine by adding a HUD, background images, particle emitters, and more in `Chapter 8`, *Polishing to a Shine – HUD, Parallax Backgrounds, Particles, and More*.

8
Polishing to a Shine - HUD, Parallax Backgrounds, Particles, and More

Our core gameplay mechanics are in place; now we can improve the overall user experience. We will turn our focus to the non-gameplay features that make our games shine. To start, we will add a **Heads-Up Display** (**HUD**) to display the player's health and coin count. Then, we will implement multiple layers of parallax background to add depth and immersion to the game world. We will also explore SpriteKit's particle system, and use a particle emitter to add production value to the game. Combined, these steps will add to the fun of the gameplay experience, invite the player deeper into the game world, and impart a professional, polished feeling to our app.

The topics in this chapter include the following:

- Adding an HUD
- Parallax background layers
- Using the particle system
- Granting safety as the game starts

Adding a HUD

Our game needs a HUD to show the player's current health and coin score. We can use hearts to indicate health – as in classic games in the past – and draw text to the screen with `SKLabelNode` to display the number of coins collected.

We will attach the HUD to the `camera` node, instead of to the scene itself, since it does not move as the player flies forward. We do not want to block the player's vision of upcoming obstacles to the right, so we will place the HUD elements in the top left corner of the screen.

When we are finished, our HUD will look like this (after the player collects 110 coins and sustains one point of damage):

First, we need to add the HUD art assets into the game. Follow these steps to add the HUD textures:

1. In Xcode, open the `Assets.xcassets` file and create a new sprite atlas by right-clicking in the left pane and selecting **New Sprite Atlas**. Name this new atlas HUD.
2. Remove the empty example sprite that Xcode creates in the new atlas.
3. In the asset pack, locate the **HUD** folder and drag its textures into your new sprite atlas, as we have done in previous chapters. When you are finished, your **HUD** atlas should look like this:

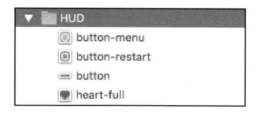

Implementing the HUD

Now that we have our art available, follow these steps to implement the HUD:

1. We will create a `HUD` class to handle all of the HUD logic. Add a new Swift file to your project, `HUD.swift`, and add the following code to begin work on the `HUD` class:

```
import SpriteKit

class HUD: SKNode {
    var textureAtlas = SKTextureAtlas(named:"HUD")
    var coinAtlas = SKTextureAtlas(named:
    "Environment")
    // An array to keep track of the hearts:
    var heartNodes:[SKSpriteNode] = []
    // An SKLabelNode to print the coin score:
    let coinCountText = SKLabelNode(text: "000000")
}
```

2. We need an initializer-style function to create a new `SKSpriteNode` for each heart shape and to configure the new `SKLabelNode` for the coin counter. Add a function named `createHudNodes` to the `HUD` class, as follows:

```
func createHudNodes(screenSize:CGSize) {
    let cameraOrigin = CGPoint(
    x: screenSize.width / 2,
    y: screenSize.height / 2)
    // --- Create the coin counter ---
    // First, create and position a bronze coin icon:
    let coinIcon = SKSpriteNode(texture:
        coinAtlas.textureNamed("coin-bronze"))
    // Size and position the coin icon:
    let coinPosition = CGPoint(x:
        -cameraOrigin.x + 23, y: cameraOrigin.y - 23)
    coinIcon.size = CGSize(width: 26, height: 26)
    coinIcon.position = coinPosition
    // Configure the coin text label:
    coinCountText.fontName = "AvenirNext-HeavyItalic"
    let coinTextPosition = CGPoint(x:
        -cameraOrigin.x + 41, y: coinPosition.y)
    coinCountText.position = coinTextPosition
    // These two properties allow you to align the
    // text relative to the SKLabelNode's position:
    coinCountText.horizontalAlignmentMode =
        SKLabelHorizontalAlignmentMode.left
    coinCountText.verticalAlignmentMode =
```

```
        SKLabelVerticalAlignmentMode.center
    // Add the text label and coin icon to the HUD:
    self.addChild(coinCountText)
    self.addChild(coinIcon)
    // Create three heart nodes for the life meter:
    for index in 0 ..< 3 {
        let newHeartNode = SKSpriteNode(texture:
            textureAtlas.textureNamed("heart-full"))
        newHeartNode.size = CGSize(width: 46,
            height: 40)
        // Position the hearts below the coins:
        let xPos = -cameraOrigin.x +
            CGFloat(index * 58) + 33
        let yPos = cameraOrigin.y - 66
        newHeartNode.position = CGPoint(x: xPos,
            y: yPos)
        // Keep track of nodes in an array property:
        heartNodes.append(newHeartNode)
        // Add the heart nodes to the HUD:
        self.addChild(newHeartNode)
    }
}
```

3. We also need a function that the GameScene class can call to update the coin counter label. Add a new function to the HUD class named setCoinCountDisplay, as follows:

```
func setCoinCountDisplay(newCoinCount:Int) {
    // We can use the NSNumberFormatter class to pad
    // leading 0's onto the coin count:
    let formatter = NumberFormatter()
    let number = NSNumber(value: newCoinCount)
    formatter.minimumIntegerDigits = 6
    if let coinStr =
        formatter.string(from: number) {
        // Update the label node with the new count:
            coinCountText.text = coinStr
    }
}
```

4. We will also need a function to update the heart graphic when the player's health changes. Add a new function to the HUD class named setHealthDisplay, as follows:

```
func setHealthDisplay(newHealth:Int) {
    // Create a fade SKAction to fade lost hearts:
    let fadeAction = SKAction.fadeAlpha(to: 0.2,
```

```
                 duration: 0.3)
        // Loop through each heart and update its status:
        for index in 0 ..< heartNodes.count {
            if index < newHealth {
                // This heart should be full red:
                heartNodes[index].alpha = 1
            }
            else {
                // This heart should be faded:
                heartNodes[index].run(fadeAction)
            }
        }
    }
}
```

5. Our HUD class is complete. Next, we will wire it up in the GameScene class. Open GameScene.swift and add a new property to the GameScene class, instantiating an instance of the HUD class:

```
let hud = HUD()
```

6. We need to add the HUD node to the camera node. Add this code at the bottom of the GameScene didMove function:

```
// Add the camera itself to the scene's node tree:
self.addChild(self.camera!)
// Position the camera node above the game elements:
self.camera!.zPosition = 50
// Create the HUD's child nodes:
hud.createHudNodes(screenSize: self.size)
// Add the HUD to the camera's node tree:
self.camera!.addChild(hud)
```

7. We are ready to send health and coin updates to the HUD. First, we will update the HUD with health updates when the player takes damage. Inside the GameScene didBegin function, locate the contact cases where the player takes damage – when he or she touches the ground or an enemy – and add this new code (in bold), which will send health updates to the HUD:

```
case PhysicsCategory.ground.rawValue:
    player.takeDamage()
    hud.setHealthDisplay(newHealth: player.health)
case PhysicsCategory.enemy.rawValue:
    player.takeDamage()
    hud.setHealthDisplay(newHealth: player.health)
```

8. Finally, we will update the HUD whenever the player collects a coin. Locate the contact case where the player contacts a coin and call the HUD setCoinCountDisplay function (new code is in bold) as follows:

```
case PhysicsCategory.coin.rawValue:
    // Try to cast the otherBody's node as a Coin:
    if let coin = otherBody.node as? Coin {
        coin.collect()
        self.coinsCollected += coin.value
        hud.setCoinCountDisplay(newCoinCount:
            self.coinsCollected)
    }
```

9. Run the project, and you should see your coin counter and health meter appear in the upper left-hand corner, as seen in the following screenshot:

Great job! Our HUD is complete. Next, we will build our background layers.

Parallax background layers

Parallax adds the *feeling of depth* to your game by drawing separate background layers and moving them past the camera at varying speeds. Very slow backgrounds give the illusion of distance, while fast moving backgrounds appear to be close to the player. We can enhance the effect by painting faraway objects with increasingly desaturated colors.

In our game, we will achieve the parallax effect by attaching our backgrounds to the scene, then slowly pushing the backgrounds to the right as the camera pans right. As the camera moves to the right (making the children of the scene appear to move left), we will move the background's x position to the right, so that the total background node movement is less than for the other children of the scene. The result will be background layers that appear to move more slowly than the rest of our game, and thus appear farther away.

In addition, each background will only be 3,072 points wide, but will jump forward at precise intervals to loop seamlessly, in a similar way to the `Ground` class.

Adding the background assets

First, add the art by following these steps:

1. Open your project's `Assets.xcassets` file in Xcode and create a new Sprite Atlas named **Backgrounds**. You can delete the empty sample sprite that Xcode creates in this new atlas.
2. In the provided game assets, locate the background images in the `Backgrounds` folder.
3. Drag and drop the eight background textures into the new **BackgroundsSprite Atlas**.

You should see the backgrounds appear in the left pane as shown here:

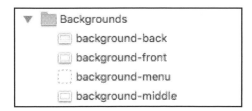

Implementing a background class

We will need a new class to manage the repositioning logic for parallax and seamless looping. We can instantiate a new instance of a `Background` class for each background layer. To create the `Background` class, add a new Swift file, `Background.swift`, to your project, using the following code:

```swift
import SpriteKit

class Background: SKSpriteNode {
    // movementMultiplier will store a float from 0-1 to indicate
    // how fast the background should move past.
    // 0 is full adjustment, no movement as the world goes past
    // 1 is no adjustment, background passes at normal speed
    var movementMultiplier = CGFloat(0)
    // jumpAdjustment will store how many points of x position
    // this background has jumped forward, useful for calculating
    // future seamless jump points:
    var jumpAdjustment = CGFloat(0)
    // A constant for background node size:
    let backgroundSize = CGSize(width: 1024, height: 768)
    // Store the Backgrounds texture:
    var textureAtlas = SKTextureAtlas(named: "Backgrounds")
    func spawn(parentNode:SKNode, imageName:String,
        zPosition:CGFloat, movementMultiplier:CGFloat) {
        // Position from the bottom left:
        self.anchorPoint = CGPoint.zero
        // Start backgrounds at the top of the ground (y: 30)
        self.position = CGPoint(x: 0, y: 30)
        // Control the order of the backgrounds with zPosition:
        self.zPosition = zPosition
        // Store the movement multiplier:
        self.movementMultiplier = movementMultiplier
        // Add the background to the parentNode:
        parentNode.addChild(self)
        // Grab the texture for this background from the atlas:
        let texture = textureAtlas.textureNamed(imageName)
        // Build three child node instances of the texture,
        // Looping from -1 to 1 so the backgrounds cover both
        // forward and behind the player at position zero.
        // closed range operator: "..." includes both endpoints:
        for i in -1...1 {
            let newBGNode = SKSpriteNode(texture: texture)
            // Set the size for this node from constant:
            newBGNode.size = backgroundSize
            // Position these nodes by their lower left corner:
            newBGNode.anchorPoint = CGPoint.zero
```

```
            // Position this background node:
            newBGNode.position = CGPoint(
                x: i * Int(backgroundSize.width), y: 0)
            // Add the node to the Background:
            self.addChild(newBGNode)
        }
    }
    // We will call updatePosition every frame to
    // reposition the background:
    func updatePosition(playerProgress:CGFloat) {
        // Calculate a position adjustment after loops and
        // parallax multiplier:
        let adjustedPosition = jumpAdjustment + playerProgress *
            (1 - movementMultiplier)
        // Check if we need to jump the background forward:
        if playerProgress - adjustedPosition >
            backgroundSize.width {
            jumpAdjustment += backgroundSize.width
        }
        // Adjust this background position forward as the camera
        // pans so the background appears slower:
        self.position.x = adjustedPosition
    }
}
```

Wiring up backgrounds in the GameScene class

We need to make three code additions to the GameScene class to wire up our backgrounds. First, we will create an array to keep track of the backgrounds. Next, we will spawn the backgrounds as the scene begins. Finally, we can call the Background class' updatePosition function from the GameScene didSimulatePhsyics function to reposition the backgrounds before every frame. Follow these steps to wire up the backgrounds:

1. Create a new array property on the GameScene class itself to store our backgrounds, as shown here:

   ```
   var backgrounds:[Background] = []
   ```

2. At the bottom of the didMove function, instantiate and spawn our three backgrounds:

   ```
   // Instantiate three Backgrounds to the backgrounds array:
   for _ in 0..<3 {
       backgrounds.append(Background())
   ```

```
    }
    // Spawn the new backgrounds:
    backgrounds[0].spawn(parentNode: self,
        imageName: "background-front", zPosition: -5,
        movementMultiplier: 0.75)
    backgrounds[1].spawn(parentNode: self,
        imageName: "background-middle", zPosition: -10,
        movementMultiplier: 0.5)
    backgrounds[2].spawn(parentNode: self,
        imageName: "background-back", zPosition: -15,
        movementMultiplier: 0.2)
```

3. Lastly, add the following code at the bottom of the `didSimulatePhysics` function to reposition the backgrounds before each frame:

```
    // Position the backgrounds:
    for background in self.backgrounds {
        background.updatePosition(playerProgress:
            playerProgress)
    }
```

4. Run the project. You should see the three background images as separate layers behind the action, moving past with a parallax effect. This screenshot shows the backgrounds as they should appear in your game:

If you are using the iOS simulator to test your game, it is normal to experience a lowered frame rate after adding these large background textures to the game. The game will still run well on physical iOS devices.

Excellent! You have successfully implemented your background system. The background makes Pierre Penguin's world feel full, adding immersion to the game. Next, we will use a particle emitter to add a trail behind Pierre – a fun addition that helps the player master the controls.

Checkpoint 8-A

To download my project to this point, visit this URL:
`http://www.joyfulgames.io/chapter-8`

Harnessing SpriteKit's particle system

SpriteKit includes a *powerful particle system* that makes it easy to add exciting graphics to your game. Particle emitter nodes create many small instances of an image that are combined together to create a great-looking effect. You can use emitter nodes to generate snow, fire, sparks, explosions, magic, and other useful effects that would otherwise require a lot of effort.

For our game, you will learn how to use an emitter node to create a trail of small dots behind Pierre Penguin as he flies, making it easier for the player to learn how their taps influence Pierre's flight path.

When we are finished, Pierre's dot trail will look something like this:

Adding the circle particle asset

Each particle system emits multiple versions of a single image in order to create a cumulative particle effect. In our case, the image is a simple circle. To add the circle image to the game, follow these steps:

1. Open the `Assets.xcassets` file in Xcode.
2. Locate the `dot@3x.png` and `dot@2x.png` images in the `Particles` folder of the downloadable game assets.
3. Drag and drop the image files into the left pane of `Assets.xcassets`.

You should see the dot sprite appear with both sizes in the right pane as shown here:

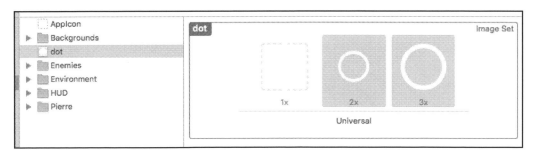

Creating a SpriteKit particle file

Xcode provides an excellent UI for creating and editing particle systems. To use the UI, we will add a new **SpriteKit Particle File** to our project. Follow these steps to add the new file:

1. Start by adding a new file to your project and locating the **SpriteKit Particle File** type. You can find this template under the **Resource** category, as shown here:

2. In the following prompt, select **Snow** as the **Particle Template**.
3. Name the file `PierrePath.sks` and click **Create** to add the new file to your project.

Xcode will open the new particle emitter in the main frame, which should look something like this:

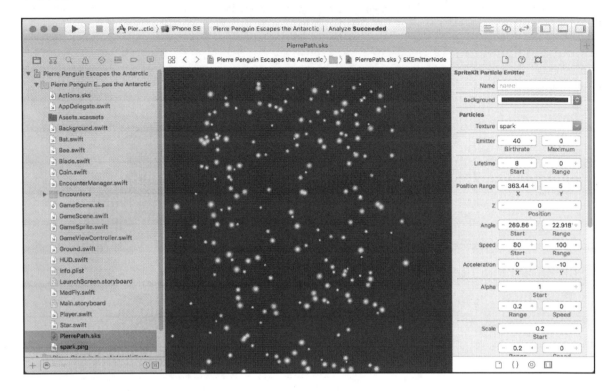

Previewing the Snow template in Xcode's particle editor

At the time of writing, Xcode's particle editor remains quirky. If you do not see the white snow particle effect in the middle, try clicking anywhere in the dark gray center area to reposition the particle emitter – occasionally it does not start where expected.

This is also useful for testing setting changes without overlap from old particles – simply click anywhere in the editor to reposition the emitter.

Make sure you have the right-hand sidebar turned on by lighting up the Utilities button in the upper right corner of Xcode, as shown here:

You can use the Utilities sidebar to edit the animation qualities of the particle emitter. You can edit several properties: the number of particles, the lifetime of a particle, how fast the particles move, how they scale up or down, and so on. This is a fantastic tool because you can see immediate feedback from your changes.

Configuring the path particle settings

To create Pierre's dot trail, update your particle settings to match the settings shown in this screenshot:

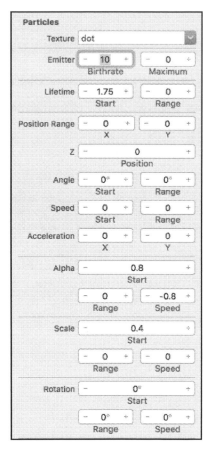

You have the correct settings when your editor shows a tiny white circle with no apparent movement.

Adding the particle emitter to the game

We will attach our new emitter to the Player node, so the emitter will create new white circles wherever the player flies. We can easily reference the emitter design we just created in the editor from our code. Open GameScene.swift and add this code at the bottom of the didMove function:

```
// Instantiate a SKEmitterNode with the PierrePath design:
if let dotEmitter = SKEmitterNode(fileNamed: "PierrePath") {
    // Position the penguin in front of other game objects:
    player.zPosition = 10
    // Place the particle zPosition behind the penguin:
    dotEmitter.particleZPosition = -1
    // By adding the emitter node to the player, the emitter moves
    // with the penguin and emits new dots wherever the player is
    player.addChild(dotEmitter)
    // However, the particles themselves should target the scene,
    // so they trail behind as the player moves forward.
    dotEmitter.targetNode = self
}
```

Run the project. You should see the white dots trailing behind Pierre, as shown here:

Good work. Now the player can see where they have flown, which is both fun and instructive. The feedback from the dots will help the player learn the sensitivity of the control system and thus master the game more quickly.

This is just one of many special effects you can create with particle emitter nodes. You can explore other creative possibilities now that you know how to create, edit, and place particle emitters in the world. Other fun ideas include sparks when Pierre bumps into enemies, and gentle snow falling in the background. We will use particles again later, when we add exploding crates to the game.

Granting safety as the game starts

You may have noticed that Pierre Penguin quickly falls to the ground as soon as you launch the game, which is not much fun. Instead, we can launch Pierre into a graceful looping arc as the game starts to give the player a moment to prepare for flight. To do so, open `Player.swift` and add this code at the bottom of the `init` function:

```
// Grant a momentary reprieve from gravity:
self.physicsBody?.affectedByGravity = false
// Add some slight upward velocity:
self.physicsBody?.velocity.dy = 80
// Create a SKAction to start gravity after a small delay:
let startGravitySequence = SKAction.sequence([
    SKAction.wait(forDuration: 0.6),
    SKAction.run {
        self.physicsBody?.affectedByGravity = true
    }])
self.run(startGravitySequence)
```

Checkpoint 8-B

To download my project to this point, visit this URL:

```
http://www.joyfulgames.io/chapter-8
```

Summary

We brought the game world to life in this chapter. We drew an HUD to show the player their remaining health and coin score, added parallax backgrounds to increase the depth and immersion of the world, and learned how to use particle emitters to create special graphics in our games. In addition, we added a small delay before gravity drags our hero down at the beginning of each flight. Our game is fun and looking great!

Next, we need a menu so we can restart the game without rebuilding the project or manually closing the application. In Chapter 9, *Adding Menus and Sounds*, we will design a start menu, add a retry button when the player dies, and play sounds and music to create a deeper gameplay experience.

9
Adding Menus and Sounds

It is easy to overlook menu design, but the menu provides your game's first impression to the player. When used correctly, your menus reinforce the brand of your game and provide a pleasant break in the action that retains the player between gameplay tries. We will add two menus in this chapter: a **main menu** that shows when the game starts, and a **retry menu** that appears when the player loses a game.

Likewise, **immersive sounds** are vital to a great game. Sound is your opportunity to support the mood of the game world and emphasize key gameplay mechanics, such as coin collecting and taking damage. Additionally, every fun game deserves addictive background music! We will add background music and sound effects in this chapter to complete the mood of the game world.

Topics in this chapter include the following:

- Building the main menu scene
- Adding the restart game menu
- Adding music with `AVAudio`
- Playing sound effects with `SKAction`

Building the main menu

We can use SpriteKit components to build our main menu. We will create a new scene in a new file for our main menu, and then use code to place a background sprite node, a logo text node, and button sprite nodes. Let's start by adding the menu scene to the project and building out the nodes.

Creating the menu scene and menu nodes

To create the menu scene, follow these steps:

1. You already added the background texture assets in Chapter 8, *Polishing to a Shine – HUD, Parallax Backgrounds, Particles, and More*. To double check, open Assets.xcassets and locate the Backgrounds Sprite Atlas. You should have a sprite called background-menu with the background textures for the menu scene. If not, you can find these two textures in the Backgrounds folder of the asset bundle.

2. Add a new Swift file to your project named MenuScene.swift.

3. Add the following code to create the MenuScene scene class:

```swift
import SpriteKit

class MenuScene: SKScene {
    // Grab the HUD sprite atlas:
    let textureAtlas:SKTextureAtlas =
        SKTextureAtlas(named:"HUD")
    // Instantiate a sprite node for the start button
    // (we'll use this in a moment):
    let startButton = SKSpriteNode()
    override func didMove(to view: SKView) {

    }
}
```

4. Next, we need to configure a few scene properties. Add this code inside the new scene's didMove function:

```swift
// Position nodes from the center of the scene:
self.anchorPoint = CGPoint(x: 0.5, y: 0.5)
// Add the background image:
let backgroundImage = SKSpriteNode(imageNamed:
    "background-menu")
backgroundImage.size = CGSize(width: 1024, height: 768)
backgroundImage.zPosition = -1
self.addChild(backgroundImage)
```

5. We need to draw the name of the game near the top of the menu. Add this code at the bottom of the `didMove` function to draw **Pierre Penguin Escapes the Antarctic**:

```
// Draw the name of the game:
let logoText = SKLabelNode(fontNamed: "AvenirNext-Heavy")
logoText.text = "Pierre Penguin"
logoText.position = CGPoint(x: 0, y: 100)
logoText.fontSize = 60
self.addChild(logoText)
// Add another line below:
let logoTextBottom = SKLabelNode(fontNamed:
    "AvenirNext-Heavy")
logoTextBottom.text = "Escapes the Antarctic"
logoTextBottom.position = CGPoint(x: 0, y: 50)
logoTextBottom.fontSize = 40
self.addChild(logoTextBottom)
```

6. Now we will add the start button. The start button is the combination of a `SKSpriteNode` for the button graphic and a `SKLabelNode` for the "`START GAME`" text. Add this code at the bottom of the `didMove` function to create the button:

```
// Build the start game button:
startButton.texture = textureAtlas.textureNamed("button")
startButton.size = CGSize(width: 295, height: 76)
// Name the start node for touch detection:
startButton.name = "StartBtn"
startButton.position = CGPoint(x: 0, y: -20)
self.addChild(startButton)

// Add text to the start button:
let startText = SKLabelNode(fontNamed:
    "AvenirNext-HeavyItalic")
startText.text = "START GAME"
startText.verticalAlignmentMode = .center
startText.position = CGPoint(x: 0, y: 2)
startText.fontSize = 40
// Name the text node for touch detection:
startText.name = "StartBtn"
startText.zPosition = 5
startButton.addChild(startText)
```

7. Finally, we will make the start button text pulse in and out to add movement and excitement to the menu. Add this code at the bottom of the `didMove` function to fade the text in and out:

```
// Pulse the start text in and out gently:
let pulseAction = SKAction.sequence([
    SKAction.fadeAlpha(to: 0.5, duration: 0.9),
    SKAction.fadeAlpha(to: 1, duration: 0.9),
    ])
startText.run(SKAction.repeatForever(pulseAction))
```

Great work! We have created our `MenuScene` class and added all the nodes we need to build the menu. Next, we will update our app to start with the menu instead of going directly to the `GameScene` class.

Launching the main menu when the game starts

So far, our app launches directly to the `GameScene` class whenever it starts. We will now update our view controller to start with the `MenuScene` class instead. Follow these steps to launch the menu when the game starts:

1. Open `GameViewController.swift` and locate the `viewWillLayoutSubviews` function.

2. Replace the entire `viewWillLayoutSubviews` function with this code:

```
override func viewWillLayoutSubviews() {
    super.viewWillLayoutSubviews()
    // Build the menu scene:
    let menuScene = MenuScene()
    let skView = self.view as! SKView
    // Ignore drawing order of child nodes
    // (This increases performance)
    skView.ignoresSiblingOrder = true
    // Size our scene to fit the view exactly:
    menuScene.size = view.bounds.size
    // Show the menu:
    skView.presentScene(menuScene)
}
```

Run the project. You should see the app start with your new main menu, which looks something like this screenshot:

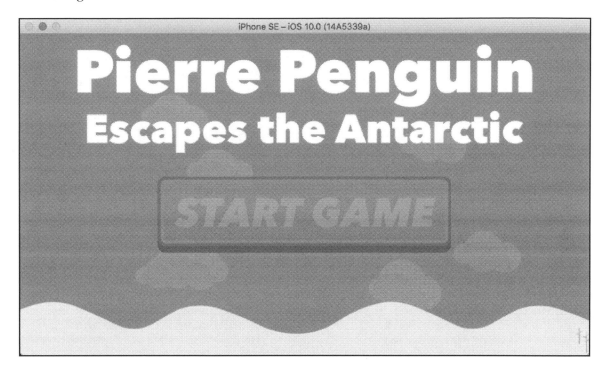

Terrific work! Next, we will wire up the **START GAME** button to transition to the GameScene class.

Wiring up the START GAME button

Just like in GameScene, we will add a touchesBegan function to the MenuScene class to capture touches on the **START GAME** button. To implement touchesBegan, open MenuScene.swift and, at the bottom of the class, add a new function named touchesBegan, as shown here:

```
override func touchesBegan(_ touches: Set<UITouch>, with event: UIEvent?) {
    for touch in (touches) {
        // Find the location of the touch:
        let location = touch.location(in: self)
        // Locate the node at this location:
        let nodeTouched = atPoint(location)
        if nodeTouched.name == "StartBtn" {
```

```
            // Player touched the start text or button node
            // Switch to an instance of the GameScene:
            self.view?.presentScene(GameScene(size: self.size))
        }
    }
}
```

Run the project and tap the start button. The game should switch to the GameScene class and gameplay will begin. Congratulations, you have successfully implemented your first main menu in SpriteKit! Next, we will add a simple restart menu that appears on top of GameScene when the player dies.

Adding the restart game menu

The restart menu is even simpler to implement. Rather than creating a new scene, we can extend our existing HUD class to display a restart button when the game ends. We will also include a smaller button to return the player to the main menu. This menu will appear on top of the action, as seen in this screenshot:

Extending the HUD

First, we need to create and draw our new button nodes in the HUD class. Follow these steps to add the nodes:

1. Open the HUD.swift file and add two new properties to the HUD class, as follows:

    ```
    let restartButton = SKSpriteNode()
    let menuButton = SKSpriteNode()
    ```

2. Add the following code at the bottom of the createHudNodes function:

    ```
    // Add the restart and menu button textures to the nodes:
    restartButton.texture =
        textureAtlas.textureNamed("button-restart")
    menuButton.texture =
        textureAtlas.textureNamed("button-menu")
    // Assign node names to the buttons:
    restartButton.name = "restartGame"
    menuButton.name = "returnToMenu"
    menuButton.position = CGPoint(x: -140, y: 0)
    // Size the button nodes:
    restartButton.size = CGSize(width: 140, height: 140)
    menuButton.size = CGSize(width: 70, height: 70)
    ```

3. We purposefully did not add these nodes as children of the HUD yet, so they will not appear on the screen until we are ready. Next, we will add a function to make the buttons appear. We will call this function from the GameScene class when the player dies. Add a function named showButtons to the HUD class, as shown here:

    ```
    func showButtons() {
        // Set the button alpha to 0:
        restartButton.alpha = 0
        menuButton.alpha = 0
        // Add the button nodes to the HUD:
        self.addChild(restartButton)
        self.addChild(menuButton)
        // Fade in the buttons:
        let fadeAnimation =
            SKAction.fadeAlpha(to: 1, duration: 0.4)
        restartButton.run(fadeAnimation)
        menuButton.run(fadeAnimation)
    }
    ```

Wiring up GameScene for game over

We need to tell the HUD class to show the restart and main menu buttons once the player runs out of health. Open GameScene.swift and add a new function to the GameScene class named gameOver, as shown here:

```
func gameOver() {
    // Show the restart and main menu buttons:
    hud.showButtons()
}
```

That is all for now; we will add to the gameOver function in the next chapter, when we implement a high score system.

Informing the GameScene class when the player dies

So far, the GameScene class is oblivious to whether the player is alive or dead. We need to change that in order to use our new gameOver function. Open Player.swift, locate the die function, and add the following code at the bottom of the function:

```
// Alert the GameScene:
if let gameScene = self.parent as? GameScene {
    gameScene.gameOver()
}
```

We access GameScene by traveling up the node tree. The Player node's parent is the GameScene class.

Run the project and die. You should see the two new buttons appear after death, as shown here:

Good work. The buttons are displaying properly, but nothing happens yet when we tap on them. To complete our restart menu, we simply need to implement tap events for the two new buttons in the GameScene class's touchesBegan function.

Implementing touch events for the restart menu

Now that our buttons are displaying, we can add touch events in the GameScene class that are similar to the **START GAME** button in the MenuScene class.

To add the touch events, open GameScene.swift and locate the touchesBegan function. We will add the restart menu code at the bottom of the for loop. I am including the entire touchesBegan function in the following code, with new additions in bold:

```
override func touchesBegan(_ touches: Set<UITouch>, with event:
    UIEvent?) {
    for touch in (touches) {
        // Find the location of the touch:
```

```
        let location = touch.location(in: self)
        // Locate the node at this location:
        let nodeTouched = atPoint(location)
        // Attempt to downcast the node to the GameSprite protocol
        if let gameSprite = nodeTouched as? GameSprite {
            // If this node adheres to GameSprite, call onTap:
            gameSprite.onTap()
        }
        // Check for HUD buttons:
        if nodeTouched.name == "restartGame" {
            // Transition to a new version of the GameScene
            // to restart the game:
            self.view?.presentScene(
                GameScene(size: self.size),
                transition: .crossFade(withDuration: 0.6))
        }
        else if nodeTouched.name == "returnToMenu" {
            // Transition to the main menu scene:
            self.view?.presentScene(
                MenuScene(size: self.size),
                transition: .crossFade(withDuration: 0.6))
        }
    }
    player.startFlapping()
}
```

To test your new menu, run the project and run out of health on purpose. You should now be able to start a new game when you die, or transition back to the main menu with a tap on the menu button. Great! You have completed the two basic menus required for every game.

These simple steps go a long way towards the overall completion of the game, and the penguin game is looking terrific. Next, we will add event sounds and music to complete the game world.

Checkpoint 9-A

Download my project to this point at this URL:

```
http://www.joyfulgames.io/chapter-9
```

Adding music and sound

SpriteKit and Swift make it very easy to play sounds in our games. We can drag sound files into our project, just like image assets, and trigger playback with `SKActionplaySoundFileNamed`.

We can also use the `AVAudio` class from the `AVFoundation` framework for more precise audio control. We will use `AVAudio` to play our background music.

Adding the sound assets to the game

Locate the `Sound` directory in the `Assets` folder and add it to your project by dragging and dropping it into the project navigator. Once you are done, you should see the `Sound` folder show up in your project just like any other file.

Playing background music

First, we will add the background music. We want our music to play regardless of which scene the player is currently looking at, so we will play the music from the view controller itself. To play the music, follow these steps:

1. Open `GameViewController.swift` and add the following `import` statement at the very top, just below the existing import lines, to allow us access to `AVFoundation` classes:

   ```
   import AVFoundation
   ```

2. Locate the `GameViewController` class and add the following property to store our `AVAudioPlayer`:

   ```
   var musicPlayer = AVAudioPlayer()
   ```

3. At the very bottom of the `viewWillLayoutSubviews` function, add this code to play and loop the music:

   ```
   // Start the background music:
   if let musicPath = Bundle.main.path(forResource:
       "Sound/BackgroundMusic.m4a", ofType: nil) {
       let url = URL(fileURLWithPath: musicPath)
       do {
           musicPlayer = try AVAudioPlayer(contentsOf: url)
   ```

```
        musicPlayer.numberOfLoops = -1
        musicPlayer.prepareToPlay()
        musicPlayer.play()
    }
    catch { /* Couldn't load music file */ }
}
```

Run the project. You should hear the background music as soon as the app starts. The music should continue as you move from the main menu to the game and back.

 If you cannot hear the music, double check that you added the Sound assets to your project as mentioned above. Also, Xcode does not get along with external speakers. Try using your Mac's internal speakers, or demo your game on a physical iOS device to troubleshoot missing sounds.

Playing sound effects

Playing simple sounds is even easier. We will use SKAction objects to play sounds on specific events, such as picking up a coin or starting the game.

Adding the coin sound effect to the Coin class

First, we will add a happy sound each time the player collects a coin. To add the coin sound effect, follow these steps:

1. Open Coin.swift and add a new property to the Coin class to cache a coin sound action:

    ```
    let coinSound =
        SKAction.playSoundFileNamed("Sound/Coin.aif",
        waitForCompletion: false)
    ```

2. Locate the collect function and add the following line at the bottom of the function to play the sound:

    ```
    // Play the coin sound:
    self.run(coinSound)
    ```

That is all you need to do to play the coin sound every time the player collects a coin. You can run the project now to test it out if you like.

 To avoid memory-based crashes, it is important to cache each `playSoundFileNamed` action object and rerun the same object each time you want to play a sound, rather than creating a new instance of a `SKAction` object for each playback.

Adding the power-up and hurt sound effects to the Player class

We will play an exciting sound when the player finds the star power-up and an injury noise when the player takes damage. Follow these steps to implement the sounds:

1. Open `Player.swift` and add two new properties to the `Player` class to cache the sound effects:

   ```
   let powerupSound =
       SKAction.playSoundFileNamed("Sound/Powerup.aif",
           waitForCompletion: false)
   let hurtSound =
       SKAction.playSoundFileNamed("Sound/Hurt.aif",
           waitForCompletion: false)
   ```

2. Find the `takeDamage` function and add this line at the bottom:

   ```
   // Play the hurt sound:
   self.run(hurtSound)
   ```

3. Find the `starPower` function and add this line at the bottom:

   ```
   // Play the powerup sound:
   self.run(powerupSound)
   ```

Playing a sound when the game starts

Lastly, we will play a sound when the game starts. Follow these steps to play this sound:

1. Open `GameScene.swift`. We will play this sound effect from the `didMove` function. Normally, it is vital to cache sound actions in a property, but we do not have to cache the game start sound because we will only play it once per scene load.

2. Add this line at the bottom of the `GameScene didMove` function:

```
// Play the start sound:
self.run(SKAction.playSoundFileNamed("Sound/StartGame.aif",
    waitForCompletion: false))
```

Great! We have added all the sound effects for our game. You can now run the project to test out each sound.

Checkpoint 9-B

Download my project to this point at this URL:

```
http://www.joyfulgames.io/chapter-9
```

Summary

We have taken huge steps towards finishing the game in this chapter. We learned how to create menus in SpriteKit, added the main menu to the game, and gave the player a way to restart the game when they run out of health. Then, we enhanced the gameplay experience with catchy background music and timely sound effects.

Next, we will explore advanced techniques you can use to make your games more fun for your players in `Chapter 10`, *Standing Out in the Crowd with Advanced Features*.

10
Standing Out in the Crowd with Advanced Features

It is important to make your game stand out if you are looking for financial success or popularity. The App Store is flooded with half-baked games. In this chapter, you will add the extra bells and whistles to our game to take it to the next level. First, we will add health power-ups so that players can heal themselves after taking damage. Then, we will add smashable crates that contain coins; nothing is more fun than smashing crates! You will learn to combine the techniques you have learned in this book to create an advanced system, and these steps will make the game feel finished and ready for players.

Topics in this chapter include the following:

- Adding fun crates to smash open
- Recycling emitter nodes with particle pools
- Creating the health power-up crate
- Spawning smashable crates that reward coins

Adding fun crates to smash open

Many classic games feature breakable crates. There is something very satisfying about flying into a crate and smashing it open. We will now add breakable crates to our game. Some of these crates will reward the player with coins, and some will reward the player with a health refill. Follow these steps to create the basic crate system:

1. Add the art assets to your project. Open `Assets.xcassets`, open the **Environment** Sprite Atlas, and drag the contents of the `Crates` folder from the downloadable asset bundle. When you are done, you should see the `crate` and `crate-power-up` appear in your Environment Atlas, as shown in the following screenshot:

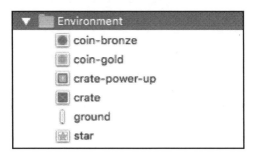

2. Open `GameScene.swift` and add a new physics category to the `PhysicsCategory` enum. We will create a physics category for crates with the value 64. When you are done, your `PhysicsCategory` enum should look like this (new code in bold):

```
enum PhysicsCategory:UInt32 {
    case penguin = 1
    case damagedPenguin = 2
    case ground = 4
    case enemy = 8
    case coin = 16
    case powerup = 32
    case crate = 64
}
```

3. Now we can add the `crate` to the `Player` class list of contact tests. This will cause a contact event to fire when the player runs into a crate. Open `Player.swift`, locate the `init` function, and update the `contactTestBitMask` to look like this (new code in bold):

```
self.physicsBody?.contactTestBitMask =
    PhysicsCategory.enemy.rawValue |
    PhysicsCategory.ground.rawValue |
    PhysicsCategory.powerup.rawValue |
    PhysicsCategory.coin.rawValue |
    PhysicsCategory.crate.rawValue
```

4. Next, we will add a new `Crate` class. Add a new `Swift` file to your project named `Crate.swift`, and add the following code:

```swift
import SpriteKit

class Crate: SKSpriteNode, GameSprite {
    var initialSize = CGSize(width: 40, height: 40)
    var textureAtlas:SKTextureAtlas =
        SKTextureAtlas(named: "Environment")
    var givesHeart = false
    var exploded = false
    init() {
        super.init(texture: nil, color: UIColor.clear,
            size: initialSize)
        self.physicsBody = SKPhysicsBody(rectangleOf:
            initialSize)

        // Only collide with the ground and other crates:
        self.physicsBody?.collisionBitMask =
            PhysicsCategory.ground.rawValue |
            PhysicsCategory.crate.rawValue
        self.physicsBody?.categoryBitMask =
            PhysicsCategory.crate.rawValue
        self.texture = textureAtlas.textureNamed("crate")
    }
    // A function to create a crate that gives health:
    func turnToHeartCrate() {
        self.physicsBody?.affectedByGravity = false
        self.texture =
            textureAtlas.textureNamed("crate-power-up")
        givesHeart = true
    }
    // A function for exploding crates!
    func explode() {
        // Do not do anything if already exploded:
```

```
            if exploded { return }
            exploded = true
            // Prevent additional contact:
            self.physicsBody?.categoryBitMask = 0
            // TODO: We will add more here in a bit
        }
        // A function to reset the crate for re-use
        func reset() {
            self.alpha = 1
            self.physicsBody?.categoryBitMask =
                PhysicsCategory.crate.rawValue
            exploded = false
        }
        // Conform to the necessary protocols:
        func onTap() {}
        required init?(coder aDecoder: NSCoder) {
            super.init(coder: aDecoder)
        }
    }
```

Excellent work; our `Crate` class is ready. Next, we will add some supporting particle effects.

Creating the Crate particle effects

We need two fun particle effects to use when the player smashes a crate. The crates that reward hearts will display a different animation than those that reward coins. First, we will create the heart particle effect by following these steps:

1. Add a new **SpriteKit Particle File** to your project (choose the bokeh particle template) and name it `HeartExplosion.sks`. You should see the particle editor open with a relaxing bokeh animation in Xcode.

2. Using the utilities bar on the right, change the particle texture to the heart-full texture and match the particle settings to this screenshot. Make sure to set **Blend Mode** to **Alpha**:

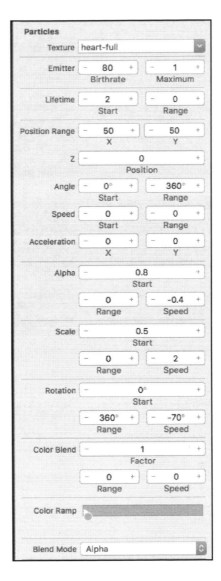

You should see a single large, rotating heart floating through the particle editor. It should look something like this:

Next, we will create the particle emitter to use when the player smashes open a crate containing coins. Follow these steps to create the emitter:

3. Add a new **SpriteKit Particle File** to your project (choose the spark particle template) and name it `CrateExplosion.sks`. You should see an exciting spark particle emitter in the editor.

4. Using the utilities bar on the right, change the particle texture to the crate texture and match the particle settings to the following screenshot. Make sure to change the **Blend Mode** to **Alpha** to get the correct crate color:

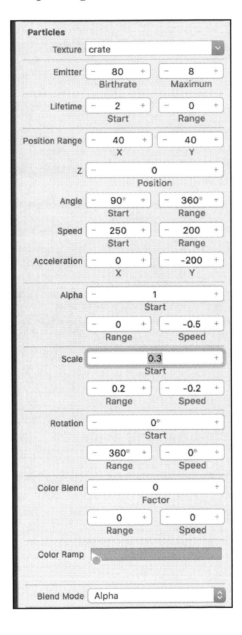

You should see small crates breaking apart and shooting off in random directions, as shown in the following screenshot:

Great! We have successfully added the particle emitters we need to create fun animations when the player smashes open our crates. Next, we will wire up the contact event and fire these animations.

Recycling emitter nodes with particle pools

We do not need to create a new emitter node for every single crate in our game. Instead, we will create a small pool of emitter nodes when the game starts and reposition them when the player smashes a crate. This is a performance best practice as emitter nodes can use system resources quickly. Follow these steps to create a particle emitter node pooling system:

1. In Xcode, create a new `.swift` file named `ParticlePool.swift`, and add the following code to your new file:

```
import SpriteKit

class ParticlePool {
    var cratePool:[SKEmitterNode] = []
    var heartPool:[SKEmitterNode] = []
    var crateIndex = 0
    var heartIndex = 0
    // A property to store a reference to the GameScene:
    var gameScene = SKScene()
    init() {
        // Create 5 crate explosion emitter nodes:
        for i in 1...5 {
            // Create a crate emitter node:
            let crate = SKEmitterNode(fileNamed:
                "CrateExplosion")!
            crate.position = CGPoint(x: -2000, y: -2000)
            crate.zPosition = CGFloat(45 - i)
            crate.name = "crate" + String(i)
            // Add the emitter to the crate pool array:
            cratePool.append(crate)
        }
        // Repeat these steps to create 1 heart emitter:
        for i in 1...1 {
            let heart = SKEmitterNode(fileNamed:
                "HeartExplosion")!
            heart.position = CGPoint(x: -2000, y: -2000)
            heart.zPosition = CGFloat(45 - i)
            heart.name = "heart" + String(i)
            heartPool.append(heart)
        }
    }
    // Called from GameScene to add emitters as children
    func addEmittersToScene(scene:GameScene) {
        self.gameScene = scene
        // Add the crate emitters to the scene:
```

```
        for i in 0..<cratePool.count {
            self.gameScene.addChild(cratePool[i])
        }
        // Add the heart emitters to the scene:
        for i in 0..<heartPool.count {
            self.gameScene.addChild(heartPool[i])
        }
    }
    // We will use this function to reposition the
    // next pooled node into the desired position
    func placeEmitter(node:SKNode, emitterType:String)
    {
        // Pull an emitter node from the correct pool:
        var emitter:SKEmitterNode
        switch emitterType {
        case "crate":
            emitter = cratePool[crateIndex]
            // Keep track of the next node to pull:
            crateIndex += 1
            if crateIndex >= cratePool.count {
                crateIndex = 0
            }
        case "heart":
            emitter = heartPool[heartIndex]
            heartIndex += 1
            if heartIndex >= heartPool.count {
                heartIndex = 0
            }
        default:
            return
        }

        // Find the node's position relative to GameScene:
        var absolutePosition = node.position
        if node.parent != gameScene {
            absolutePosition =
                gameScene.convert(node.position, from:
                    node.parent!)
        }
        // Position the emitter on top of the node:
        emitter.position = absolutePosition
        // Restart the emitter animation:
        emitter.resetSimulation()
    }
}
```

2. Open `GameScene.swift` and initialize your `ParticlePool` class as a new property on the `GameScene` class:

```
let particlePool = ParticlePool()
```

3. In the `GameScene` class, locate the `didMove` function. At the bottom of the function, call the `ParticlePool.addEmittersToScene` function to add our emitter nodes to the `GameScene` node tree:

```
// Add emitter nodes to GameScene node tree:
particlePool.addEmittersToScene(scene: self)
```

4. Perfect! Now we can simply call the `placeEmitter` function whenever we want to display a `HeartExplosion` or `CrateExplosion` emitter animation.

Checkpoint 10-A

Download my project up to this point from the following URL:
`http://www.joyfulgames.io/chapter-10`

Wiring up crate contact events

Now we can fire custom logic whenever the player runs into a crate. We will place our particle effect and award health or coins. Follow these steps to wire up the contact event:

1. In Xcode, open `GameScene.swift` and locate the `didBegin` function, where we set our physics contact logic.
2. We need to call the `explode` function on our `Crate` class any time the player runs into a `Crate`. Add a new case for crate contact below the star `powerup` contact case, as shown here (new code in bold):

```
case PhysicsCategory.powerup.rawValue:
    player.starPower()
case PhysicsCategory.crate.rawValue:
    if let crate = otherBody.node as? Crate {
        // Call the explode function with a reference
        // to the GameScene:
        crate.explode(gameScene: self)
    }
```

3. Before we can award health, we need to add a new property to the `Player` class to set a maximum amount of health. Open `Player.swift` and add a new property called `maxHealth`, shown in the following snippet (new code in bold):

```
var health:Int = 3
let maxHealth = 3
```

4. Open `Crate.swift` and expand the `explode` function to place a particle emitter and reward coins or health as follows:

```
func explode(gameScene:GameScene) {
    // Do not do anything if this crate already exploded:
    if exploded { return }
    exploded = true
    // Place a crate explosion at this location:
    gameScene.particlePool.placeEmitter(node: self,
        emitterType: "crate")
    // Fade out the crate sprite:
    self.run(SKAction.fadeAlpha(to: 0, duration: 0.1))

    if (givesHeart) {
        // If this is a heart crate, award a health point:
        let newHealth = gameScene.player.health + 1
        let maxHealth = gameScene.player.maxHealth
        gameScene.player.health = newHealth > maxHealth ?
            maxHealth : newHealth
        gameScene.hud.setHealthDisplay(newHealth:
            gameScene.player.health)
        // Place a heart explosion at this location:
        gameScene.particlePool.placeEmitter(node: self,
            emitterType: "heart")
    }
    else {
        // Otherwise, reward the player with coins:
        gameScene.coinsCollected += 1
        gameScene.hud.setCoinCountDisplay(newCoinCount:
            gameScene.coinsCollected)
    }
    // Prevent additional contact:
    self.physicsBody?.categoryBitMask = 0
}
```

5. Since we are fading our crates to fully transparent, we will need to add code in the `EncounterManager` to call the `Crate` class `reset` function when it recycles an encounter and resets the crate nodes. Open `EncounterManager.swift` and locate the `resetSpritePositions` function. Underneath the line that resets the `zRotation`, try to cast the node as a `Crate` and call the `reset` function (new code in bold):

```
// Reset the rotation of the sprite:
spriteNode.zRotation = 0
// If this is a Crate, call its reset function:
if let crateTest = spriteNode as? Crate {
    crateTest.reset()
}
```

We are now ready to use our crate system. Next, we will add a health crate that randomly spawns after encounters.

Adding a health crate

We have taken many steps to create our crate system. Now we can add our first crate: a crate in the `GameScene` class that will award health points to the player. Follow these steps to wire up the heart crate:

1. In `GameScene.swift`, instantiate a new instance of the `Crate` class as a property of the `GameScene`:

```
let heartCrate = Crate()
```

2. At the bottom of the `GameScene` `didMove` function, add the `heartCrate` to the node tree and call the function that makes it award a heart:

```
// Spawn the heart crate, out of the way for now
self.addChild(heartCrate)
heartCrate.position = CGPoint(x: -2100, y: -2100)
heartCrate.turnToHeartCrate()
```

3. Locate the `GameScene.didSimulatePhysics` function. Find the code that spawns the power-up star. We can add on to this code to spawn our heart crate randomly after some encounters. Add the following code below the `starRoll` conditional (new code in bold):

```
// Each encounter has a 10% chance to spawn a star:
let starRoll = Int(arc4random_uniform(10))
if starRoll == 0 {
    // Note: all of the power-up star code is still here
    // I'm excluding it here for brevity.
}
if starRoll == 1 {
    // Position the heart crate after this encounter:
    heartCrate.reset()
    heartCrate.position = CGPoint(x:
        nextEncounterSpawnPosition - 600, y: 270)
}
```

We should now be randomly spawning our heart crate 10% of the time. You may wish to change the conditional to check if `starRoll` is greater than zero for testing purposes temporarily (so it will spawn the heart crate 90% of the time). Just remember to change it back when you finish testing. Go ahead, run your project, and crash into a heart crate. You should gain a health point and see the awesome result of our hard work, shown here:

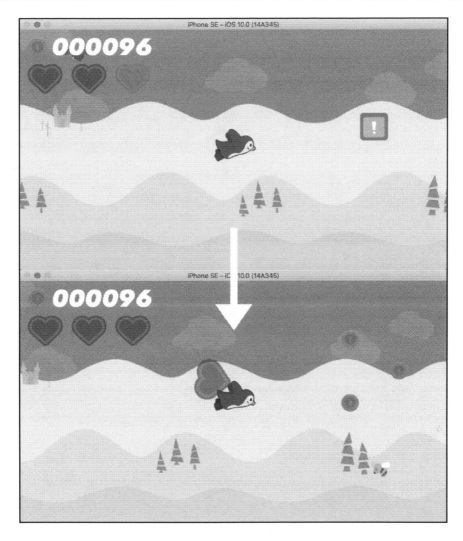

Great work! Next, let's add some smashable coin crates for the player to break apart.

Smashing coin crates

To add smashable coin crates, we will create new crate sprites in our encounters using the scene editor. Follow these steps to add a `Crate` to the game:

1. In Xcode, open one of the encounter scenes we created earlier in this book. I am using `EncounterA.sks` for this example. The scene will open in the **Scene Editor**. In the lower right, click on the Media Library to see the media assets in your project.

2. Locate the crate texture and drag it into your encounter.

3. In the upper right, click on the **Custom Class** Inspector and assign a **Custom Class** of `Crate`, as illustrated in the following screenshot:

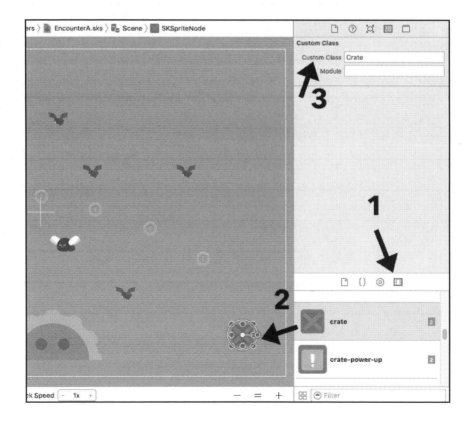

4. Repeat the process to create as many crates as you like. You can place them slightly above the ground and gravity will settle them into place.

You can always hold option and drag an existing sprite to create a clone with the same properties (persisting the **Custom Class** setting).

That is all you need to do to add smashable crates to the game. You can repeat this in all of your encounters to fill out crates throughout your game. My example scene ended up looking like this:

Run your project and try flying into some crates. You should see the crates smash apart and your coin score increase! Your smashable crates should look like this when you fly into them:

Checkpoint 10-B

Download my project up to this point from the following URL:
http://www.joyfulgames.io/chapter-10

Summary

Great work! We have added a fun component to our game and learned some advanced techniques. We created a multiuse Crate class, wired it up for contact events, and created new animations with particle emitters. We learned an advanced technique to recycle our emitter nodes with a pool of particle emitters. Then, we used our new systems to create a smashable health crate and crates that reward the player with coins.

Our game is looking great and is a lot of fun to play! In Chapter 11, *Choosing a Monetization Strategy*, we will discuss publishing, advertising, and monetization options.

11
Choosing a Monetization Strategy

It is a great time to be an indie game developer. There are an abundance of monetization options and game marketplaces. We can easily connect our projects with people looking to play our genre and style. To stand out, you will need to spend time and energy on marketing your project while considering alternate routes such as crowdfunding.

There are more freemium games than ever before; it is now very possible to make money strictly from ad revenue or in-app purchases. Additionally, options exist to enlarge your market by making your app available in other regions. You can set yourself up for success by considering the market and aligning your game's style to the paying demand that exists. It is also important to manage your projects wisely so you can complete and publish your games. Each of these topics is very deep, but we will spend time exploring the basics to give you an idea of how to spend your marketing time.

Topics in this chapter include:

- Developing your marketing plan
- Leveraging crowdfunding
- Showing display ads for revenue
- Selling in-app purchases
- Localization into foreign markets
- Managing scope and completing projects

Developing your marketing plan

Indie game development has never been more accessible. This is fantastic news, but it also means that we face a sea of noise and competition when we try to attract attention to our efforts. Further complicating matters, creating and executing a marketing plan requires different skills than those required to create a video game. Many developers would rather spend their time coding or drawing versus building awareness through social outreach. Luckily, there are many resources available to help us get started.

When to start marketing

Many games have their best sales day on the day they are launched. This means that you need to start building public awareness of your project early in development so your popularity peaks as you release your game. You need to time your publicity to coincide with your release date in order to maximize your sales window.

As soon as you have some representative material, publish it! Take it to social media, Reddit, and game forums. You will get valuable feedback and start to create awareness around your project. The indie developer community is very friendly and welcoming of new material.

Marketing checklist

Here are some proven steps to build awareness around your game and yourself as an indie developer:

- **Website and development blog:** You will need a basic website so that you show up in search engine results. It is beneficial to keep a regular development blog where you post about interesting challenges you are solving or simply share your latest progress. Though it can be hard to spend time on writing a blog post instead of implementing a new system in your game, it will pay off as you build a fan base and awareness. For instance, my development blog lead to me writing this book!

- **Social Media**: The game developer community on Twitter is bursting with activity. Engaging with other developers on Twitter is a fantastic way to gauge interest in your genre and spread awareness of your project. Try to build authentic relationships with other members to grow your fan base. This can pay off if someone with a large following retweets a post about your game. And if you are using hash tags (such as #gamedev) to spread awareness, try to time your posts during Twitter's busiest hours – usually weekends and evenings.

- **Video trailers**: On OSX, you can use QuickTime to easily record screen-capture videos and then edit them with iMovie. You do not need anything fancy, just a simple video showing off the unique mechanics and fun of your game. Post your trailers to YouTube and link them from Twitter and your developer blog. Additionally, you can take small snippets and make gifs to share. Gifs are one of the best formats to communicate your game quickly.

- **Screenshot Saturday**: `#screenshotsaturday` is a widely used hashtag in the indie game community. You can find it on Twitter, Facebook, Reddit (a weekly thread in /r/gamedev), and others. You should definitely be making gifs of your weekly progress and sharing them with the community each Saturday. It is a fun way to get feedback and create buzz.

- **Game journalists and blogs:** Cold calling journalists, a socially awkward activity, does not come easily to many game developers. However, it is vitally important to get the exposure from features on game websites and blogs, especially leading up to your launch date. One article on the right blog can be your primary source of traffic. There is no perfect formula, but try to reach out to blogs that write about similar games and genres, be friendly and humble, and make sure to give them plenty of material to write about. You can also create an easy to use press kit that you can hand off with all of the relevant information a journalist will need to write a story.

- **presskit():** presskit() is a simple, open source tool to generate a press-ready site where you can consolidate media and information about your game to distribute to journalists. Many game journalists will already be familiar with this format, which may make things easier for them. Making it easy for a journalist or blogger to write about you is a winning strategy. You can find presskit() at `http://dopresskit.com/`.

Leveraging crowdfunding

Many developers are turning to **crowdfunding** platforms such as **Kickstarter** and **IndieGoGo** to fund their projects. These sites allow you to put your unfinished product before the world and ask supporters to chip in monetarily to make it a reality. You ask for a small amount of money from a great number of people. This is an excellent way to gather funds if your idea resonates well with the public.

Crowdfunding opens up many new possibilities, but the successful crowdfunding campaigns create their own success by hyping their projects through the press and social media. Crowdfunding campaigns that launch with pre-existing fan bases are most likely to succeed.

Pros and cons of crowdfunding

One of the best aspects of crowdfunding is that it forces developers to create all the necessary marketing materials for their games. Even if your crowdfunding campaign is unsuccessful, you will gain all the materials and assets you need to market your game in the process. On the other hand, you will need to devote extensive time to your campaign, potentially distracting from development (especially if you are a solo developer).

Crowdfunding campaigns need a lot of outside publicity to be successful. Simply having a Kickstarter page is not enough to get a campaign noticed. The campaigns that manage to attract the attention of the game media are the campaigns that gain traction. Once you do have some awareness, however, you may gain extra press just for having a crowdfunding campaign running.

An additional advantage to crowdfunding is that it lets you quickly test the demand for your genre and style of game. If you are able to find backers for your project, it is likely something that gamers are willing to purchase. This bodes well for the financial success of your game.

If you do decide to use crowdfunding, spend some time researching campaigns that succeeded and try to mimic what they did well. Crowdfunding takes serious time and effort; do not expect it to be an easy source of money. It pays off if you are able to communicate a great idea and find a willing group of fans who are looking for what you are making.

Showing display ads for revenue

The iOS App Store market favors free games that show ads or provide in-app purchases to make money. Free games tend to get more attention than games that cost money up front, and going with a freemium model is a good idea if you do not already have massive exposure for your project. Mobile advertising is a large, growing business; there are plentiful options if you choose to shows ads in your games.

The upsides to showing ads

Ads can be the most straightforward approach to monetizing your game, assuming you can build the traffic volume to make an impact. Here are some reasons to use ads in your game:

- When done right, users do not mind ads. Some developers are working them into the gameplay by giving in-game rewards for watching a video ad. This seems to be a winning formula: it results in a higher revenue per user, and users are generally not annoyed by this style of ad. Unity conducted a study that showed, *71 percent of players choose watching video ads as their preferred way to 'pay' for game content* (full study available here: `http://response.unity3d.com/in-game-advertising-the-right-way-monetize -engage-retain-whitepaper`).

- Ads do not take much development work, compared to quality in-app purchases. All you need to do is configure and implement your ad networks (the companies you partner with to deliver your ad content) and you are free to focus on making the best game possible. Contrast that with the work of constantly creating new game content to sell to your players in small bits, even after launch, for in-app purchases. Most ad networks provide an SDK to speed up the implementation process.

- Ads allow you to provide your full game up front and free, meaning you will receive more installs and your players will get to use the full game without limits or additional purchases (unless you choose to use both ads and in-app purchases together). Free games receive a tremendous increase in downloads over games that charge, so allowing your players to download your game freely is a solid strategy if you do not have an existing fan base.

The downsides to showing ads

There are definitely reasons to skip the ad networks and choose another monetization strategy, including:

- Showing ads can damage your own brand–especially banner ads that take up screen real estate during gameplay. Misuse of ads makes a game look cheap and mass produced. Think about how your ads may influence your fans' view of your game itself, assuming you want to carry a fan base forward to your next game.
- Ads can be annoying if implemented hastily. If you do choose to use ads, please do so in a tactful manner. For instance, interstitial video ads between levels are less offensive than ads that take up screen space during gameplay.
- You need a high volume of players to make ads lucrative. No monetization strategy succeeds without volume, but ads are particularly worthless if you cannot generate a thriving fan base.
- If you do choose to go with ads, you can choose from many ad networks. New ad networks are constantly springing up, while many developers are finding success with some of the most popular networks (such as **Google's AdMob** and **Chartboost**).

Selling in-app purchases

In-app purchases have grown at an astounding rate since Apple launched the App Store. Love them or hate them, in-app purchases are a winning monetization strategy that works for many developers and companies. When implemented well, in-app purchases encourage players to spend extra time with your game and explore every expanse and subplot.

On the other hand, in-app purchases can corrupt gameplay for the sake of monetization. There are entire books on the subject of using psychological gameplay tricks to keep players hooked on in-app purchases, and we have seen this style used a lot in the App Store (with financial success). Still, it is possible to create an in-app purchase system that is both successful and healthy for your players. Let us explore some strategies.

In-app purchase strategies

Successfully implementing an in-app purchase system is a very deep topic, but we will briefly examine some proven strategies:

- Make sure to provide enough free content that your players are hooked and are willing to pay more for additional levels, skins, or game time on top of the already solid foundation of gameplay.
- If you allow players to work towards in-app purchases using in-game currency, randomize the rewards they receive in game. Randomized rewards are more compelling and keep the player hooked, hoping for the chance of a great reward roll on their next opportunity.
- Provide samples of in-app purchasable content. By mixing purchasable content into free gameplay, users will learn how the special content works and will be more interested in purchasing it.
- If you have a semi-successful in-app purchase game, keep developing! Once you have proven that gamers are interested in paying for your system, you are likely to make more money by adding onto the existing game than by starting a new project. This means that if you choose in-app purchases, you should continue to support your existing games with new content buildout after launch.
- Run daily features, limited time content, and sales around holidays. These types of sales tactics work to gain more purchases.

A word about farming your players

Without getting too philosophical, I prefer not to use gameplay-based in-app purchases because they create a conflict of interest for the game developer. Rather than focusing on creating a great game, you are incentivized to create a game that evokes specific psychological and emotional responses in your players in order to prompt repeated purchases. Some of that is true for any monetization strategy, but in-app purchases in particular can end up dictating gameplay design in order to make the most money.

Localization into foreign markets

While localization can be expensive, it can also open up an entirely new market for your game, which has a multiplying effect on your user base. You may want to consider translating your game into other languages, especially if your game does not use many words.

Sometimes localization requires more than just language translation. Games in English can usually be literally translated to mainstream European languages and find success, but countries such as China or Japan can be more difficult. Besides cultural differences, these countries have strong game development industries already, and it can be tough to gain attention. Still, the market is massive and it may be worth the effort.

Despite the high level of effort and possibility of mistakes, expanding into new markets can quickly multiply the number of people who are potentially interested in your project. It is worth a look, especially once you have proven that your game has demand in the marketplace. For indies, localization is likely most practical for simpler puzzle games and more difficult for storied games where cultural differences will take extra work and care.

Managing scope and completing projects

Finishing and publishing projects is hard for everyone. Video games are expansive works of art and even simple games can take months to polish. The success stories in the media often portray a lone developer making millions of dollars with their first idea, but that is not often the reality. Rather than attaching to one idea, most pros build many quick prototypes and iterate on their best ideas. It is like any artistic endeavor – who ends up the better painter: the student who takes thirty days to meticulously paint one picture, or the student who paints a new picture every day for thirty days? The student who paints 30 paintings has the opportunity to learn far more.

It is for this reason that I recommend starting with simple puzzle games. Make a snake clone, a Tetris clone, and a gem game clone. If you can finish and publish these simple games, you are probably in great shape to take on more challenging artistic pursuits. You will become a better game maker with every game you make, so do not worry about making the perfect game on your first try.

I also recommend building out a menu system that you can reuse between your different projects. It is easy to finish gameplay, work on a game, and then let the project languish because working on menus and title sequences is tedious (at least for me). Make the dull work as easy as possible for yourself and you will have a much better chance of success.

Finally, stay organized. Use pen and paper, create time charts, plan your schedule, and measure yourself against your plans. Make a list of everything you need to do to finish your game (including your marketing efforts) and assign a day and time to tackle each task. Assigning a specific time to tasks is far more effective than simply dumping items onto a to-do list.

Summary

We have learned about the basic approaches to marketing our games and finding players interested in our projects. This can be a challenging area for indie developers. While some industry pros recommend spending as much time on your marketing as you do making your game, coding and art probably comes more easily than cold calling journalists or hiring translators. However, marketing is a necessary part of successful indie game publishing. This marketing work gives you the best chance of success when you publish your game.

I hope that this chapter gave you some ideas on how to build a fan base. First, we looked at the basic checklist of a solid marketing plan. Then, we explored how to approach crowdfunding. Third, we looked at using ads to generate revenue, and contrasted that to selling in-app purchases. Fourth, we took a brief look at the power of localization and exposing your games to new markets. Finally, we reviewed some useful tips for making sure you bring your games to completion and publication. In the next chapter, we will return to Xcode and wire up Game Center to our penguin game for leaderboards and achievements.

12
Integrating with Game Center

Apple provides an online social gaming network called **Game Center**. Your players can share high scores, track achievements, challenge friends, and start matchmaking for multiplayer games with Game Center. In this chapter, we will use Apple's iTunes Connect website to register our app with Apple. Then, we can integrate with Game Center to add leaderboards and achievements in our game.

 You will need an active Apple developer account (which costs $99 per year) to register your app with Apple, access the iTunes Connect website with Game Center, and publish your game to the App Store.

The topics in this chapter include:

- Registering an app with iTunes Connect
- Authenticating the player's Game Center account in our app
- Opening Game Center from the MenuScene class
- Adding a leaderboard
- Creating and awarding achievements

Registering an app with iTunes Connect

Since Apple will be storing our high scores and achievements on their centralized servers, we need to communicate to Apple that we need Game Center for our app. The first step is to create a record for our app on the iTunes Connect website. Follow these steps to create an iTunes Connect record:

1. Use Safari and navigate to `http://itunesconnect.apple.com`.
2. Sign in with your Apple developer account information.

3. When you reach the iTunes Connect dashboard, click on the **My Apps** icon.

4. Towards the upper-left, click on the + symbol and select **New iOS App**, as shown in the following screenshot:

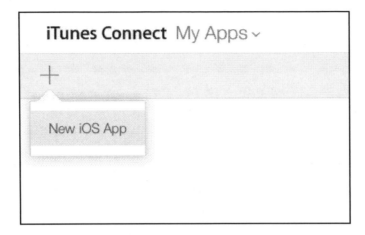

5. In the subsequent dialog, locate the link at the bottom that says **Register a new bundle ID on the Developer Portal**. Click this link to create a Bundle ID for your app.

6. You will arrive in the developer portal. Select **App IDs** in the left-hand column, under the **Identifiers** column, as shown in the following screenshot:

7. Click on the plus icon in the upper-right corner to add a new iOS App ID. You will land on a page titled Registering an App ID. This page may appear overwhelming at first, but you only need to fill out two fields.

8. First, enter the name of your app in the **App Description** section.

9. Scroll down to the **App ID Suffix** section. Make sure to select **Explicit App ID** and then enter the **Bundle ID** field from your Xcode project settings, as shown here:

App ID Suffix

○ **Explicit App ID**

If you plan to incorporate app services such as Game Center, In-App Purchase, Data Protection, and iCloud, or want a provisioning profile unique to a single app, you must register an explicit App ID for your app.

To create an explicit App ID, enter a unique string in the Bundle ID field. This string should match the Bundle ID of your app.

Bundle ID: | io.JoyfulGames.PierrePenguin |

We recommend using a reverse-domain name style string (i.e., com.domainname.appname). It cannot contain an asterisk (*).

10. Scroll down to the **App Services** section and double-check that the **Game Center** option is already checked.

11. At the bottom of the page, click **Continue**. Then click **Register** on the subsequent confirmation page.

12. You should see a **Registration Complete** page. You can now close this tab and return to iTunes Connect, picking up where you left off on the new iOS app screen.

It can take some time before the **Bundle ID** you just created shows up in iTunes Connect. If this happens, take a break and try again after a few moments.

13. Enter the **Name** of your app, the **Primary Language**, the **Version**, and **SKU** (which is for your internal use and not visible to the public). Then select the Bundle ID you just created, as shown in the following screenshot:

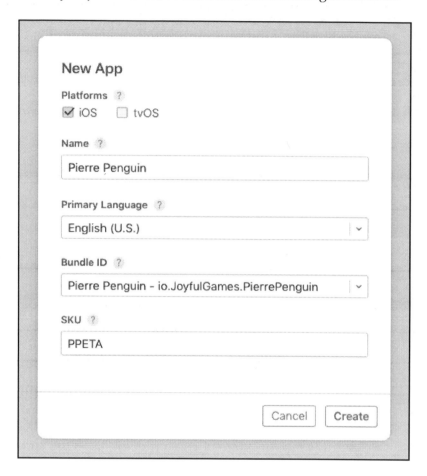

14. Click **Create** in the lower-right. You should now see an overview of your app in iTunes Connect, which will look something like the following screenshot:

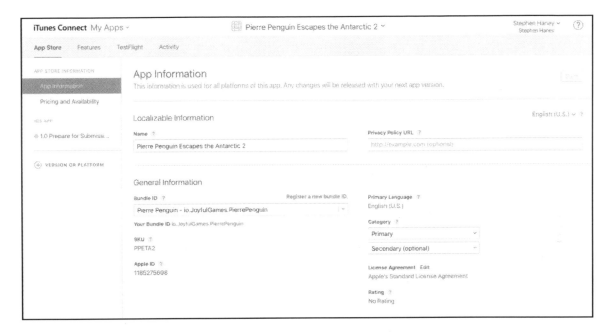

Congratulations, not only are we close to configuring Game Center, we have also taken the first step towards preparing our app for submission to the App Store!

Creating a test user

We have informed Apple that we want to use Game Center in our game. Next, we need to create a sandbox user account for testing purposes.

Game Center uses separate test servers during app development, so we will not be able to use our real Apple ID to log in to Game Center while we are testing. Instead, we will create a sandbox account in iTunes Connect.

 The iOS Developer Library states, *Always create new test accounts to test your game in Game Center. Never use an existing Apple ID.*

Follow these steps to create a Game Center sandbox account for testing:

1. On the iTunes Connect home page, select **Users and Roles**, as shown in the following screenshot:

2. Once you are on the **Users and Roles** page, click on **Sandbox Testers** in the navigation bar at the top of the screen.
3. As directed on the **Sandbox Testers** page, click the + icon to add a new user.

4. Fill out the test user's information to your liking. Here is how I filled out my test user's information:

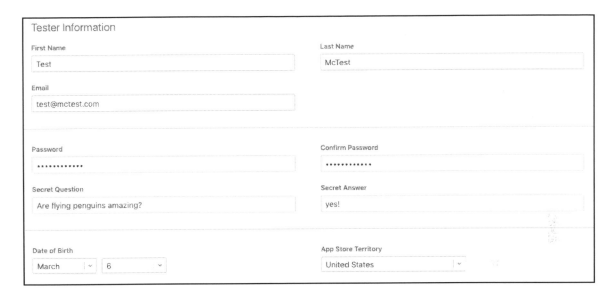

5. Click the **Save** button to create the new user.

Make sure to keep your live Apple ID and your sandbox account separate. The sandbox account will become invalid if you use it to log in to a live Game Center app.

Great! The next step is to integrate Game Center with our game code. We will start by authenticating the player's Game Center account when they open our app.

Authenticating the player's Game Center account

As soon as our app starts, we will check if the player is already logged in to their Game Center account. If not, we will give them a chance to log in. Later, when we want to submit high scores or achievements, we can use the authentication information we gathered when the app launched, instead of interrupting their gaming session to collect their Game Center information.

Follow these steps to authenticate the player's Game Center account when the app starts:

1. First, we will turn on Game Center for your project in Xcode. Open the **Capabilities** tab of your project settings and make sure Game Center is flipped to **ON**, as shown in the following screenshot:

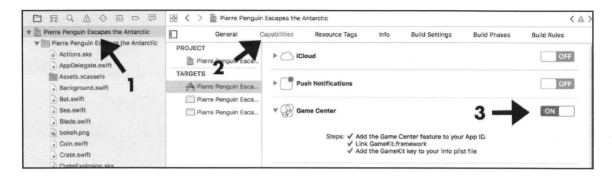

2. We will now be working in the `GameViewController` class, so open `GameViewController.swift` in Xcode.

3. Add a new `import` statement at the top of the file so we can use the `GameKit` framework:

```
import GameKit
```

4. In the `GameViewController` class, add a new function called `authenticateLocalPlayer` with this code:

```
// (We pass in the menuScene instance so we can create a
// leaderboard button in the menu when the player is
// authenticated with Game Center)
func authenticateLocalPlayer(menuScene:MenuScene) {
    // Create a new Game Center localPlayer instance:
    let localPlayer = GKLocalPlayer.localPlayer()
    // Create a function to check if they authenticated
    // or show them the log in screen:
    localPlayer.authenticateHandler =
        {(viewController, error) -> Void in
        if viewController != nil {
            // They are not logged in, show the log in:
            self.present(viewController!, animated: true,
                completion: nil)
        }
        else if localPlayer.isAuthenticated {
            // They authenticated successfully!
            // We will be back later to create a
```

```
                    // leaderboard button in the MenuScene
            }
            else {
                // Not able to authenticate, skip Game Center
            }
        }
    }
```

5. At the bottom of the `GameViewController` class `viewWillLayoutSubviews` function, add a call to the new `authenticateLocalPlayer` function you just created:

```
authenticateLocalPlayer(menuScene: menuScene)
```

Run your project. You should see Game Center animate in, asking for your credentials, as shown in the following screenshot:

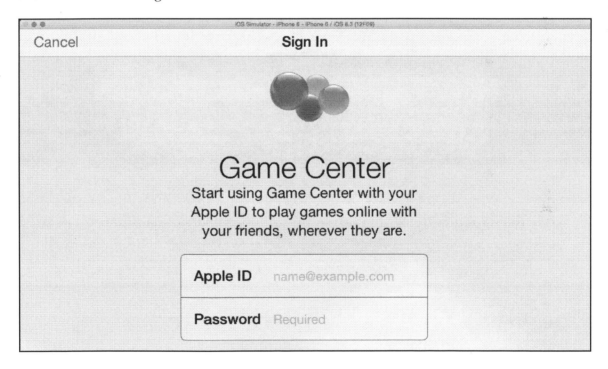

Great! Remember to use your new sandbox account. The first time you log in, Game Center will ask a few extra questions to set up your account. Once you finish with the Game Center form, you should return to the main menu, with a small banner animating in and out from the top of the screen, letting you know you are signed in. The banner looks something like this:

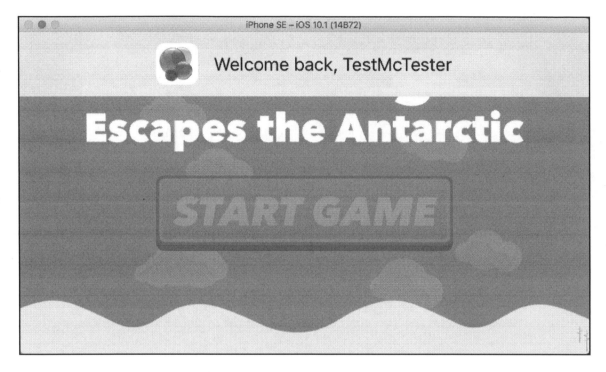

If you see this welcome back banner, you have successfully implemented the Game Center authentication code. Next, we will add a leaderboard button to the menu so the player can see their progress within our app.

Opening Game Center in our game

If the user is authenticated, we will add a button to the MenuScene class so they can open the leaderboard and view achievements from within our game. Alternatively, players can always use the Game Center app in iOS to view their progress.

Follow these steps to create a leaderboard button in the menu scene:

1. Open `MenuScene.swift` in Xcode.

2. Add a new import statement at the top of the file so we can use the `GameKit` framework:

   ```
   import GameKit
   ```

3. Update the line that declares the `MenuScene` class so that our class adopts the `GKGameCenterControllerDelegate` protocol. This allows the Game Center screen to inform our scene when the player closes the Game Center:

   ```
   class MenuScene: SKScene, GKGameCenterControllerDelegate {
   ```

4. We need a function that will create the leaderboard button and add it to the scene. We will call this function once the Game Center authenticates the player. Add a new function to the `MenuScene` class, named `createLeaderboardButton`, as shown in the following snippet:

   ```
   func createLeaderboardButton() {
       // Add some text to open the leaderboard
       let leaderboardText = SKLabelNode(fontNamed:
           "AvenirNext")
       leaderboardText.text = "Leaderboard"
       leaderboardText.name = "LeaderboardBtn"
       leaderboardText.position = CGPoint(x: 0, y: -100)
       leaderboardText.fontSize = 20
       self.addChild(leaderboardText)
   }
   ```

5. We will call our `createLeaderboardButton` function from the `didMove` function if the player is already authenticated with Game Center. This creates the button for players who return to the main menu after playing a game. Add the following code to the bottom of the `didMoves` function:

   ```
   // If they're logged in, create the leaderboard button
   // (This will only apply to players returning to the menu)
   if GKLocalPlayer.localPlayer().isAuthenticated {
       createLeaderboardButton()
   }
   ```

6. Next, we will create the function that actually opens the Game Center. Add a new function named showLeaderboard, as shown in the following snippet:

```
func showLeaderboard() {
    // A new instance of a game center view controller:
    let gameCenter = GKGameCenterViewController()
    // Set this scene as the delegate (helps enable the
    // done button in the game center)
    gameCenter.gameCenterDelegate = self
    // Show the leaderboards when the game center opens:
    gameCenter.viewState =
        GKGameCenterViewControllerState.leaderboards
    // Find the current view controller:
    if let gameViewController =
        self.view?.window?.rootViewController {
        // Display the new Game Center view controller:
        gameViewController.show(gameCenter, sender: self)
        gameViewController.navigationController?
            .pushViewController(gameCenter, animated: true)
    }
}
```

7. We need to add another function to adhere to the GKGameCenterControllerDelegate protocol. This function is named gameCenterViewDidFinish, and the Game Center will invoke it when the player clicks the Done button in Game Center. Add the function to the MenuScene class, as shown in the following snippet:

```
// This hides the game center when the user taps 'done'
func gameCenterViewControllerDidFinish
    (_ gameCenterViewController:
    GKGameCenterViewController) {
    gameCenterViewController.dismiss(animated: true,
        completion: nil)
}
```

8. To wrap up the MenuScene code, we need to check for taps on our leaderboard button in the touchesBegan function to invoke showLeaderboard. Update the touchesBegan function if block, as shown in the following snippet (new code in bold):

```
if nodeTouched.name == "StartBtn" {
    self.view?.presentScene(GameScene(size: self.size))
}
else if nodeTouched.name == "LeaderboardBtn" {
    showLeaderboard()
```

```
        }
```

9. Next, open `GameViewController.swift` and locate the `authenticateLocalPlayer` function.

10. Update the block where the player authenticated successfully to call our new `createLeaderboardButton` function in the `MenuScene` class. This creates the leaderboard button for newly authenticated people as they start the app. The code is shown here (new code in bold):

```
else if localPlayer.authenticated {
    // They authenticated successfully
    menuScene.createLeaderboardButton()
}
```

Good work. Run the project and you should see a leaderboard button appear in the menu after Game Center authenticates, as shown in the following screenshot:

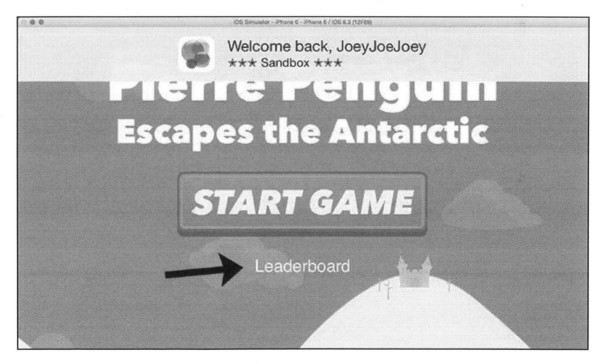

Terrific–if you tap on the **Leaderboard** text, Game Center will open within the game. Now your players will be able to view leaderboards and achievements directly from your game. Next, we will create a leaderboard and an achievement in iTunes Connect to populate Game Center.

Checkpoint 10-A

To download my project up to this point, visit the following URL:

```
http://joyfulgames.io/chapter-10/.
```

Adding a leaderboard of high scores

We will submit the player's scores to the Game Center servers every time they finish a game. The first step is to register a new leaderboard on iTunes Connect.

Creating a new leaderboard in iTunes Connect

First, we will create our leaderboard in iTunes Connect. We can then connect to this leaderboard from our code and send new scores. Follow these steps to create the leaderboard record in iTunes Connect:

1. Log back in to iTunes Connect and navigate into the Game Center page for your app.
2. Locate and click the button that says **Add Leaderboard**.
3. The next page asks you what type of leaderboard you want to create. Choose **Single Leaderboard**.
4. Fill out the information for your leaderboard. You can reference my example here:

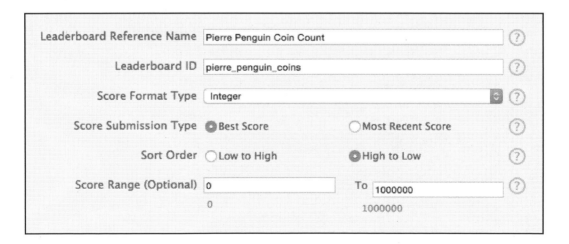

Let's take a look at each field:

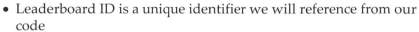

- Reference Name is a name used internally for leaderboard listings in iTunes Connect
- Leaderboard ID is a unique identifier we will reference from our code
- Score Format Type describes the type of data you will be passing in (most commonly integer data for high scores)
- Normal leaderboards use a Score Submission Type of Best Score, with a Sort Order of High to Low
- Score Range is an anti-cheating measure you can use to block obviously false scores from showing up on the leaderboard

5. Next, click on the **Add Language** button. You will choose a name and score formatting for your leaderboard on this screen. These fields are largely self-explanatory, but you can reference my example here:

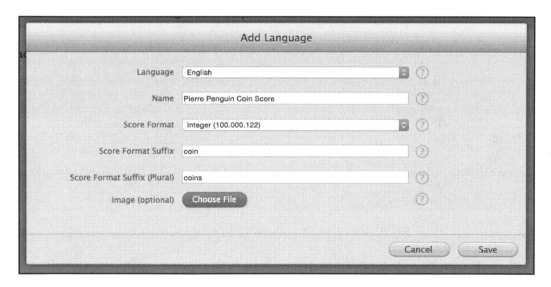

6. Click **Save** twice (once for the language dialog and once on the leaderboard screen).

You should be back on the Game Center page with your new leaderboard listed in the leaderboards section. Next, we will push new scores into the leaderboard from our game code.

Updating the leaderboard from the code

It is simple to send a new score to the leaderboard from the code. Follow these steps to send the number of coins collected to the leaderboard every time a game ends:

1. In Xcode, open `GameScene.swift`.

2. Add an import statement at the top so we can use the `GameKit` framework in this file:

   ```
   import GameKit
   ```

3. Add a new function in the `GameScene` class named `updateLeaderboard`, as shown here:

   ```
   func updateLeaderboard() {
       if GKLocalPlayer.localPlayer().isAuthenticated {
           // Create a new score object, with our leaderboard:
           let score = GKScore(leaderboardIdentifier:
               "pierre_penguin_coins")
           // Set the score value to our coin score:
           score.value = Int64(self.coinsCollected)
           // Report the score (wrap the score in an array)
           GKScore.report([score], withCompletionHandler:
               {(error : Error?) -> Void in
                   // The error handler was used more in old
                   // versions of iOS, it would be unusual to
                   // receive an error now:
                   if error != nil {
                       print(error!)
                   }
           })
       }
   }
   ```

4. In the `GameScene` class `GameOver` function, call the new `updateLeaderboard` function:

   ```
   // Push their score to the leaderboard:
   updateLeaderboard()
   ```

Run the project and play through a game to send a test coin score to the leaderboard. Then, tap back to the menu scene and click the **Leaderboard** button to open Game Center within your game. You should see your first score appear on the leaderboard! It will look something like this:

 Sometimes it can take a minute before your score shows up on the leaderboard. If you can't see your score, try restarting the simulator before troubleshooting your code.

Great work–you have implemented your first Game Center leaderboard. Next, we will follow a similar series of steps to create an achievement for collecting 200 coins in one game.

Adding an achievement

Achievements add a second layer of fun to your game and create replay value. To demonstrate a Game Center achievement, we will add a reward for collecting 200 coins without dying.

Creating a new achievement in iTunes Connect

Just like the leaderboard, we first need to create an iTunes Connect record for our achievement. Follow these steps to create the record:

1. Log into iTunes Connect and navigate to the Game Center page for your app.
2. Underneath the leaderboards list, locate and click the **Add Achievement** button.
3. Fill out the information for your achievement. Here are my values:

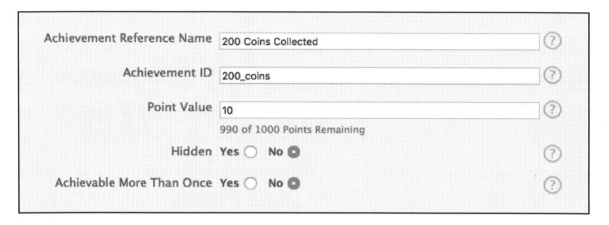

Let's take a look at each field:

- Reference Name is the name iTunes Connect will use internally to refer to the achievement
- Achievement ID is the unique identifier we will use to reference this achievement in our code
- You can assign a Point Value to each achievement so players can earn more achievement points as they collect new achievements
- Hidden and Achievable More Than Once are self-explanatory, but you can use the question mark buttons on the right for additional information from Apple

4. Click the **Add Language** button. We will name the achievement and give it a description, as in the leaderboard process. Additionally, an image is required for achievements. The image dimensions can be *512 x 512* or *1024 x 1024*. You can find the one I used in our Assets bundle download, in the `Extras` folder, `gold-medal.png`. Here are my values:

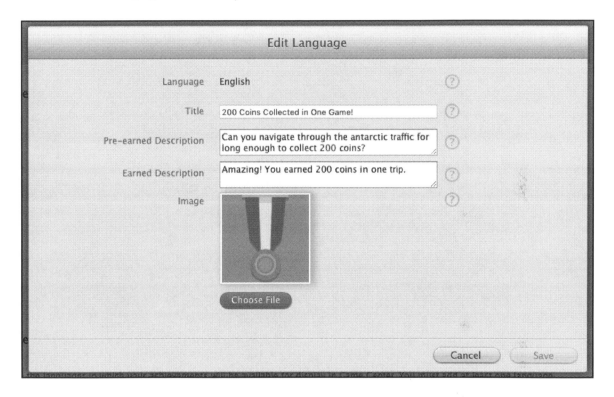

5. Click **Save** twice (once for the language dialog and once on the achievement screen).

Terrific, you should be back on the main iTunes Connect Game Center page for your app with your new achievement listed in the Achievements section. Next, we will integrate this achievement into the game.

Updating achievements from the code

Much like sending leaderboard updates, we can send achievement updates to Game Center from GameScene. Follow these steps to integrate our 200 coin achievement:

1. Open GameScene.swift in Xcode.

2. If you skipped over the leaderboard section, you will need to add a new import statement at the top of the file so we can use GameKit. If you have already implemented the leaderboard, you can skip this:

   ```
   import GameKit
   ```

3. Add a new function to the GameScene class, named checkForAchievements, as shown in the following snippet:

   ```
   func checkForAchievements() {
       if GKLocalPlayer.localPlayer().isAuthenticated {
           // Check if they earned 200 coins in this game:
           if self.coinsCollected >= 200 {
               let achieve = GKAchievement(identifier:
                   "200_coins")
               // Show a notification that they earned it:
               achieve.showsCompletionBanner = true
               achieve.percentComplete = 100
               // Report the achievement!
               GKAchievement.report([achieve],
                   withCompletionHandler:
                   {(error : Error?) -> Void in
                       if error != nil {
                           print(error!)
                       }
               })
           }
       }
   }
   ```

4. At the bottom of the gameOver function, invoke the new checkForAchievements function:

   ```
   // Check if they earned the achievement:
   checkForAchievements()
   ```

Run the project and, if you dare, complete a 200 coin fly through. When your game ends, you should see a banner proclaiming your new achievement conquest, as shown in the following screenshot:

Great work! You have implemented Game Center leaderboards and achievements into your game.

Checkpoint 10-B

To download my project up to this point, visit the following URL:

```
http://joyfulgames.io/chapter-10/.
```

Summary

Integrating with Game Center is a great feature for your players. In this chapter, we learned how to create an iTunes Connect record for our app, authenticate Game Center users in our code, create new leaderboards and achievements on iTunes Connect, and then integrate those leaderboards and achievements within our game. We have made a lot of progress!

We are officially finished working on the game itself. In the next chapter, we will prepare our app for publication, upload the code for Apple to review, and revisit what we have learned while creating our great game. Everything is coming together and we are ready to take the final step towards publishing our game. Congratulations!

13
Ship It! Preparing for the App Store and Publication

What a grand journey! We have stepped through each component of the game development process in Swift and we are finally ready to share our hard work with the world. We need to prepare our project for publication by finishing the assets associated with it: the assorted app icons, the launch screen, and the screenshots for the App Store. Then, we will fill out the description and information for our app in iTunes Connect. Finally, we will use Xcode to upload a production archive build and submit it to the Apple review process. We are very close to seeing our game in the App Store!

While I can show you the general path that you can use to submit your app, this process is constantly changing as Apple updates iTunes Connect. In addition, every app has unique aspects that may require a variation on the path I demonstrate in this chapter. I encourage you to browse Apple's official documentation in the iOS Developer Library and refer to Stack Overflow for updated answers. You can locate the iOS Developer Library by browsing to `https://developer.apple.com/reference`.

Topics in this chapter include:

- Finalizing assets: app icons and the launch screen
- Finalizing iTunes Connect information
- Configuring pricing
- Uploading our project from Xcode
- Submitting for review in iTunes Connect

Finalizing assets

There are several peripheral assets that we need before we can publish our game. We will create a set of app icons, redesign the launch screen, and take screenshots for each device we support for the App Store previews.

Adding app icons

Our app requires multiple sizes of our app icon to display correctly in the App Store and the various iOS devices we support. You can find a sample icon set in the provided assets bundle, in the `Icon` folder.

 You should design your icon to be 1024 pixels wide by 1024 pixels tall and then resize down for the other variations. Make sure to check each variation to ensure it looks good after resizing. You will upload this large size directly to iTunes Connect later in this chapter.

The best way to integrate your icons into your project is to use the `Assets.xcassets` asset bundle, preconfigured for app icons, that comes along with new projects. We will drag and drop our icons into this file to bring them into the project.

Follow these steps to add our icons to the project:

1. In Xcode, open the `Assets.xcassets` file and locate the **AppIcon** image set in the left pane.
2. Drag and drop the images from the assets bundle into the corresponding icon slots. You can drag your files in as a group and Xcode will process them into the correct slots. You can ignore the icon slots for the Settings icons, since our app does not integrate with iOS settings. When you are finished, your icon image set will look something like the following screenshot:

3. Go into your general project settings by clicking on your project in the project navigator. Locate the **App Icons Source** setting and make sure it is set to **AppIcon** to use the image bundle, as shown in the following screenshot:

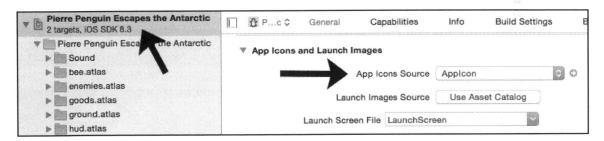

We are finished adding our icons in Xcode. We will need to upload a few more icon sizes to iTunes Connect later. You can run your project on a real device to see your new icons in action.

Designing the launch screen

When a user taps your icon on their device, iOS shows your app's launch screen as an extremely fast-loading, simple preview. This creates the illusion that your app loads almost instantly. The player gets immediate feedback from their tap while your app actually loads in the background. This is not the place to add logos, branding, or information of any kind. The goal is to create a very simple screen that looks like your app before the content is in place. For Pierre Penguin, we will implement a simple, blank, sky blue background that looks like the main menu before it has any content.

Follow these steps to set up your sky blue launch screen:

1. Open the `LaunchScreen.storyboard` file in Xcode. You will see the launch screen open in the interface builder.
2. Make sure you have your Utilities bar open on the right-hand side of Xcode, and open the **Attributes Inspector**, as demonstrated here:

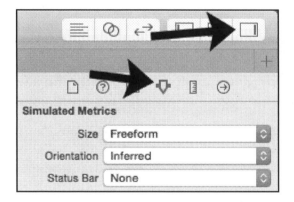

3. Locate the background color setting in the right bar, and then click on the existing white color option to open a color selection window.
4. Choose the color sliders tab, and enter the RGB value 102, 153, 242, as shown here:

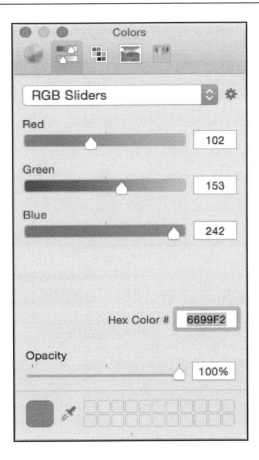

5. You should see the entire frame turn the sky blue color from our game.

6. Next, enter your project general settings by clicking the project name in the project navigator. As you did before for the app icons, make sure the **Launch Screen File** setting is **LaunchScreen.storyboard**:

Perfect! When we run our app, we will see the sky blue color immediately, providing a smoother transition between the home screen and our fully loaded app.

Taking screenshots for each supported device

Fun screenshots will make your game stand out in the App Store. I created some sample screenshots for Pierre Penguin in the assets bundle's `Screenshots` folder. You will need to create separate screenshots for each iOS device you want to support.

Screenshots must be JPG or PNG files. You only need to upload the largest phone size and largest tablet size if you would like your screenshots to be automatically resized down. Or, you can create individual screenshots for each size. For our example, I'll be uploading a 5.5" iPhone screenshot and a 12.9" iPad screenshot and allowing iTunes Connect to automatically resize for other devices.

This table describes the various sizes that you can create:

Device size	Screenshot size for a full screen game
3.5" (required)	960×640 pixels
4" (required)	1136×640 pixels
4.7"	1334×750 pixels
5.5"	2208×1242 pixels
iPad 9.7"	2048×1536 pixels
iPad 12.9"	2732×2048 pixels

Once your screenshots are prepared, you are ready to finalize your game settings in iTunes Connect. We will complete the iTunes Connect details next.

Finalizing iTunes Connect information

iTunes Connect controls our app's details in the App Store. We will use iTunes Connect to create a description for our game, add the screenshots we want to display in the App Store, and configure our pricing information and project settings.

Follow these steps to fill out your iTunes Connect information:

1. Open the iTunes Connect website in Safari. Browse to the **My Apps** section, and then click on your game. iTunes Connect will take you to the **App Information** tab of your game's page.

2. Click on the **Prepare for Submission** section in the left navigation bar, under the **iOS APP** heading.

3. We will start with the screenshots. Drag and drop each device screenshot into the corresponding slot in the **App Video Preview and Screenshots** section, as shown in the following screenshot:

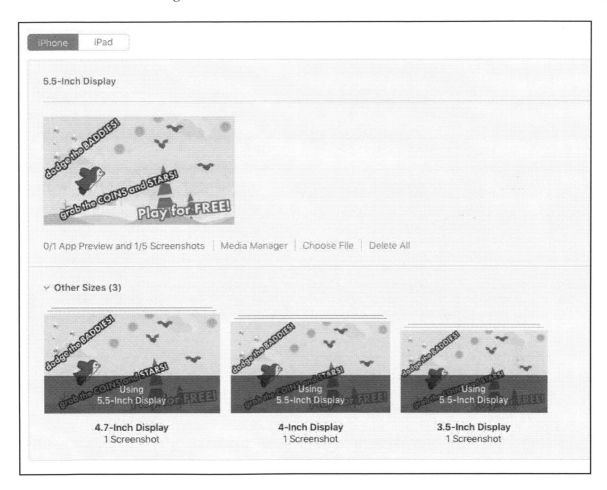

4. Scroll down and fill out the information in the next section: **Name**, **Description**, **Keywords**, and associated URLs. These fields are self-explanatory, but you can always click on the small gray question mark circles for detailed information from Apple.

A word on keywords: users will find your app more easily if you have strong, accurate keywords. Try to use phrases you think people may type in to the App Store that should lead them to your game. You are limited to 100 characters, so omit spaces between keywords.

5. Next, scroll down to the **General App Information** section. Here you will upload your app icon, enter a version number (1.0), pick the App Store category for your app (**Games**), and provide your address information. Again, click on the gray question mark circles if you need further information on any of these fields.

6. Scroll down and locate **Game Center**, then flip the slider to the on position. You will need to add your leaderboard and achievements by clicking the blue plus icons, as shown in the following screenshot:

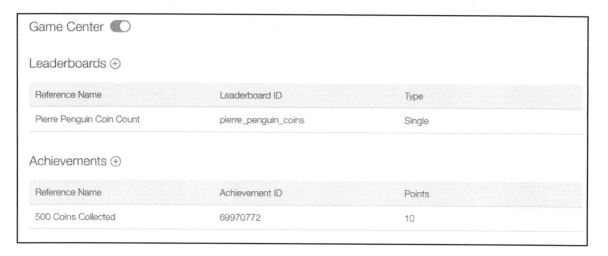

7. Finally, scroll to the **App Review Information** section and fill out your contact information again. This is for the Apple employee reviewing your app in the event they need more information. You can also select whether you want your game to release to the App Store automatically after approval, or wait for you to release it manually, later, to coincide with your marketing efforts.

8. Click on **Save** in the upper-right corner.

Configuring pricing

Pierre Penguin is going to be free for all to play, but you can choose from many pricing strategies for your games.

Apple is constantly updating iTunes Connect and the pricing section changes often. Your experience may not match these steps exactly.

Follow these steps to set the price for your game:

1. On the iTunes Connect page for your game, click the **Pricing and Availability** link in the left navigation bar.
2. Choose a **Price Tier**, **Availability**, and educational discount. Here are some sample settings for reference:

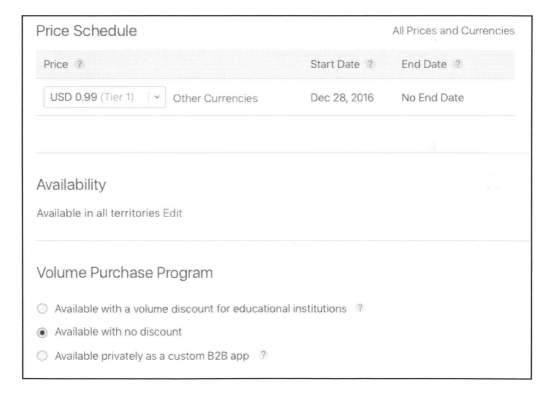

3. Click on **Save** in the upper-right.

Perfect! Our iTunes Connect information is complete and ready to submit to the App Store review process. Now we just need to finalize and upload our build in Xcode.

If you want to charge for your game then you will need to fill out the contracts and banking information found in the **Agreements, Tax, and Banking** section of iTunes Connect.

Uploading our project from Xcode

Next, we will create a final build of our game, validate that it contains everything it needs for the App Store, and upload the bundle to iTunes Connect.

First, we will create the deployment archive for our game. When you are happy with your project, use the **Product** menu and select **Archive…**, as shown in the following screenshot:

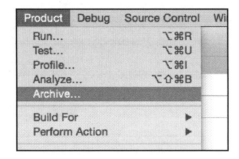

If **Archive…** is grayed out, make sure to select a real iOS device or the **Generic iOS Device** option in the target scheme drop-down in the upper-left of Xcode.

Once the process finishes, Xcode will open your archive list. From here, you can validate your app to make sure it includes all the requisite assets and profiles it needs to be on the App Store. Follow these steps to validate your app and upload it to iTunes Connect:

1. Click on the **Validate** button, as shown in the following screenshot, to validate your app:

2. The following screen will ask you to choose a development team for your app. If you are a solo developer, you will simply select your own name, as shown in the following screenshot:

3. Xcode will create a distribution provisioning profile for you, and then take you to a summary screen. Simply click the **Validate** button:

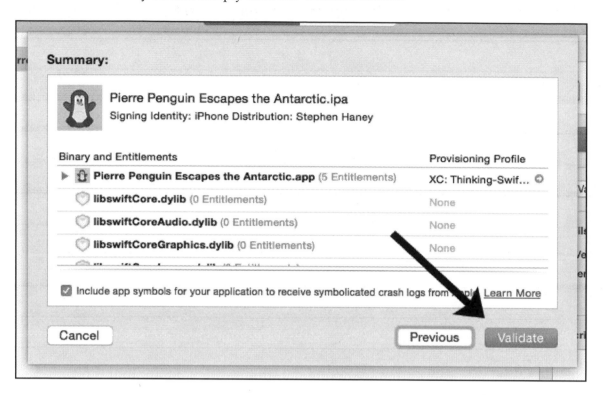

4. Xcode will proceed to validate that everything is ready for the App Store, which may take a few moments. After it completes, you should see a success message, as shown in the following screenshot. If you receive any errors, you may be missing an asset or profile that the App Store requires. Read and respond to the error message, and refer to the iOS Developer Library, Internet searches, or Stack Overflow for further assistance:

5. Click **Done**, and then click the blue **Submit to App Store** button to upload the archive to iTunes Connect, as shown in the following screenshot:

6. You will need to click through the validate steps again, and then finally click **Upload**. Xcode will then upload your app to iTunes Connect and display another success message.

Congratulations! You have successfully uploaded your app to Apple. We are almost finished submitting our app. Next, we will return to iTunes Connect to push our app into the review and approval process.

Submitting for review in iTunes Connect

We have finished prepping our project and we are now ready to push our hard work into the Apple review process. Follow these steps to submit your app to Apple:

1. Return to the iTunes Connect website and browse to your game's page (on the **iOS App Prepare for Submission** section in the left navigation bar).

2. Scroll down to the **Build** section, and select **Click + to add a build before you submit your app.**

Build ⊕

Select a build before you submit your app.

Submit your builds using Xcode 6 or later, or Application Loader 3.0 or later.

---

3. Use the radio button to select the archive you just uploaded, and then click **Done**, as shown in the following screenshot. It can take a few minutes (or sometimes hours) for the uploaded build to show in this list:

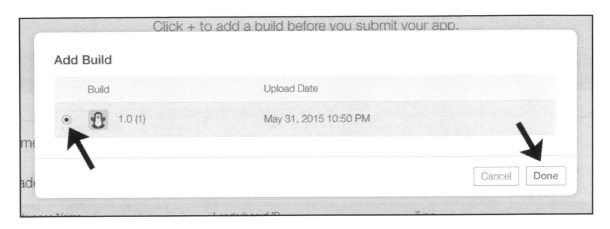

4. Click **Save** in the upper-right corner and the **Submit for Review** button should light up in blue:

5. Click **Submit for Review** and iTunes Connect will show the **Submit for Review** page with three final questions about your game. Apple wants to know if your app uses cryptography, third-party content, or advertising. I answered no to all three questions for Pierre Penguin. It is important to answer these questions accurately, so use the question mark icons in iTunes Connect for more information if you are unsure on how to proceed.

6. After you answer the **Submit for Review** questions, click on **Submit** in the upper right. This is the final step of the submission process.

If your app submits successfully, iTunes Connect will return to the iOS App section. You will see the app status change to **Waiting For Review**, as shown here:

Terrific! We have submitted our game to Apple. It is typical for the review process to take 7-14 days. Do not be discouraged if your game comes back without approval, Apple commonly requires developers to correct small issues and resubmit their apps. You are on your way to seeing your game in the App Store!

Summary

Many indie developers struggle with the final steps of publishing their games. If you are ready to publish a game, you are doing a great job! In this chapter, we created app icons and our launch screen, finalized our App Store marketing information in iTunes Connect, used Xcode to archive and upload our game, and submitted our game to Apple for review. You should now be confident in your ability to publish your games to the App Store.

We accomplished a great deal throughout the course of this book: we assembled a complete Swift game from a new project template to publication. As we go our separate ways, I wish you tremendous luck in your future game development endeavors. My hope is that you are now confident in starting your own game projects with Swift. I look forward to seeing your creations in the App Store!

Index

COUNTY COLLEGE OF MORRIS
LEARNING RESOURCE CENTER
214 CENTER GROVE ROAD
RANDOLPH, NJ 07869

Made in the USA
Middletown, DE
21 October 2018